Dedication

*For each human being
who faithfully lives each day
in search of his or her truest self.*

Growing Up Together

A Spiritual Perspective for Parents of Adolescents

DAVID WALSH

Illustrations by Martha Campbell.

Cover and book design by Julie Van Leeuwen.
Cover illustration by Martha Campbell.

SBN 0-912228-73-3

©1980 St. Anthony Messenger Press.
All rights reserved.
Printed in the U.S.A.

Contents

Introduction: Putting Parenting in Spiritual Perspective . . 1

Part One: Growth Begins Within

1. Parenting Without Parentheses
   The Art of Listening. 9

2. Recognizing the Adolescent in in Ourselves
   The Art of Adult Behavior 23

Part Two: Spelling Out the Meaning of P-A-R-E-N-T

3. **P** is for Patience
   The Art of Losing Your Mind . . . 39

4. **A** is for Anger
   The Art of Affirming Your Adolescent 55

5. **R** is for Religion
   The Art of Believing 69

6. **E** is for Environment
   The Art of Living 'in the Midst of' the World. 85

7. **N** is for Needs
   The Art of Separating Wants From Needs 101

8. **T** is for Touch
   The Art of Being God's Instrument . 111

Appendix: Books to Help Parents on Their Way 120

accident; each event is a God-event. So it is from God that you and your children have come together.

You are, therefore, the perfectly matched family. From this perspective your child is perfect whether he or she is brilliant or bullheaded, your pride and joy or your constant heartbreak. And you, with your failings and strengths, are the perfect parent.

To human eyes you and your offspring may seem ill-matched; but in the eyes of God, the

God who sees all of reality and not merely the fragments seen by human minds, you and your children are meant for each other. Together you will grow in holiness (that is, grow *up*), or you and they will remain emotionally and spiritually stunted.

This eternal perspective is important to remember on days when your perfect angel seems particularly possessed by some demon. As you grow in wisdom you will be able to see how your adolescent's antics have called forth from you an inner strength you had not suspected you possessed. You will discover that you have grown and, in effect, that you have been *raised* by your children.

I have dealt with parents and adolescents as a parish priest and secondary school teacher, and I have had to deal with my own inner struggle to "grow up" during the past several years living a contemplative life-style. The insights shared in these pages have no other authority than the authority of these personal experiences.

I was encouraged that these reflections may be of some value to you as a parent by a remark from a mother of four, three of whom are teenagers, after she read a copy of Chapter 3. Reflecting on my status as non-parent, she commented, "How does he know all this? He doesn't have any kids." Then she added wonderingly, "Or does he?"

The answer to her question is *yes* and *no*. I do not have children in the sense of having sired a son, but I do have an inner child and adolescent with whom I have to deal daily. More will be said about these "persons" in the following chapter.

For now let me say that, for me, parenting is not, technically speaking, a problem. My problem is *parents*—not because parents are problems *to me* but *to themselves*. Most parents I know feel merely inadequate when it comes to rearing small and middle-aged children; but when it comes to raising an adolescent, many enter into a state most aptly called shock.

Parents of young adults may know that one day their son or daughter will turn out all right, but they are not all that convinced they will live to see it! The day these stunned parents "come to," they will realize with inexpressible joy they already have.

Parents and those of us who find ourselves in the role of "parent teacher" can together progress in age and wisdom. Our progress demands that we attempt a spiritual journey into the lives of the adolescents in our midst and into our own adolescent selves.

Chapter 2 of this book will present and attempt to explain the terms of Transactional Analysis (TA) in an easily understandable form. A clear grasp of TA terminology will make the remaining chapters of the book more comprehensible.

Beginning, then, with Chapter 3 we will discuss parental patience (P), adult anger (A), real religion (R), environmental control (E), necessary needs (N) and, finally, a most important topic, keeping in touch (T). By thus dissecting the word *P-A-R-E-N-T*, we will attempt to understand what Chapter 1 refers to as "parenting without parentheses."

All of this, of course, is offered with full awareness that the only universal rule for parents is written on the fleshy tablets of your hearts. Together you, father and mother, have the knowledge and the wisdom to nurture the growth of your children. But you must get in touch with this knowledge each day and in every situation. Then your united hearts will *know* the correct thing to do, say, permit.

After reflecting on the art of parenting, only one thing can be said with absolute certainty: It can never be gotten down to a science.

Jesus reprimanded his disciples' *scientific* approach to the children clamoring for his attention and affection. Jesus gathered the children to himself even though his disciples espoused the principle that children are to be seen and not heard. According to Jesus, the children's "freshness" (as unique messengers of the Divine in our species) was the quality required for entry into the Kingdom. Jesus tells us it is "to such as these" that the Kingdom belongs.

We daily pray as a Christian people, "Thy Kingdom come." If God's Kingdom is to come, it will be by your child learning to become his or her unique self. As parents, therefore, you are being invited, in an awesome manner, to accept the daily challenge to do God's will on earth. And your task begins at home.

1. The Art of Listening

Parenting Without Parentheses

Parentheses are a way of further clarifying what has already been said. Parenthetical phrasing is poor literary style. Parentheses (a form of punctuation used to enclose a parenthetical expression) exhaust (that is, tire out) the reader (the person who is currently looking at and digesting the material). Painful isn't it?

For an adolescent to have two living parentheses (parent-theses) on duty full-time, always trying to clarify or qualify his or her identity, may be more than painful. Such pressure may be destructive. Just as too many parenthetical thoughts can cause the main idea to be forgotten, too much parenthetical parenting can cause an adolescent's real personality to get lost in the shuffle.

What happens if your teenage son decides to drop his baseball glove on third base and don a pair of ballet slippers? His action might do violence to your idea of proper masculine activity. Your concept of your son does not mesh with the human being standing in leotards before you. Your parentheses are thrown out of kilter. You may be tempted to squeeze your son into your perspective.

But if you can stop and listen, really listen, to your son you will be in a position to help him grow. You can help him understand the "whys" of his actions. He might genuinely be another Rudolf Nureyev, or he might be canceling out a potential major league contract due to a fleeting frustration.

Your temptation to squeeze your offspring into your own parentheses comes from a desire to help them in life. You want to tell them the "right" thing to do "for their own good." This well-meaning love prompts all parental proddings.

But some of our "well-meaning love" is generated by our *own* needs rather than our children's—and that's the part that needs monitoring. Whether these parental needs are obvious or subtle, they form a sort of static that keeps you from seeing your children's unique possibilities, from helping them hear their unique word spoken by God.

Parental static can come disguised in sheep's

clothing. What may appear as a desire to "motivate" your adolescent to use his or her talents might be a subtle way of "keeping up with the Joneses" or attaining a success missed in your own adolescence. Constant parental self-examination will lower the number of times you add your own unresolved emotional burdens to the already sloping shoulders of your son or daughter.

Adolescents need parents whose parentheses are more *open* than *closed*. Open parentheses make parents hearing and responsive—like two gigantic "ears." The bigger the better.

Look at your son, then, from this perspective. He is straddled between third base and the spotlight at the New York City Ballet. Your son needs you to lend him your ears, not to squeeze him into your closed parentheses about who and what he should be. Parenting within the confines of parentheses keeps a young person from speaking his or her piece in this most puzzling of worlds.

Recently I heard about a woman who was a wonderful parent. Whether or not this woman was a mother herself, she certainly contributed to giving birth to a child-like part of a man we all know. As a history teacher she promoted this young man not on the basis of his academic acumen but because, as she put it, "The world needs *humor* more than it does *history teachers.*" The man was the late Edgar Bergen.

Perhaps Bergen was a dummy when it came to history. No doubt many of his instructors felt he was spending too much time playing with "toys." Fortunately he had one history teacher who was capable of seeing *beyond*—beyond convention, beyond the "way things are supposed to be."

This woman with deep insight saw beyond the *fact* of a poor history student to the *potential* of a great entertainer. I, for one, feel a sense of gratitude to this woman who looked beyond what a high school student *ought* to be to what this uniquely tailored human being actually *was*.

The type of vision this "parent" had is the kind all parents must develop. When adolescents are trapped in their own idea of what they ought to be, or in *your* idea about them, they are blind to their potential. They will grow only if you can see *beyond*, and help them see *beyond*.

A Word-Made-Flesh

Your adolescent's special word was made

flesh in a mother's womb. This word-made-flesh is the result of that tremendous creative love between the two people we now call parents. You made the flesh; God created the spirit. We marvel at this young human being, aware that we know nothing of how wonderfully he or she is made.

From the first day you view your child, you turn to others in the medical profession and ask, "Is she okay?" Then you listen attentively to her voice during the day or his breathing at night to see if this magnificent machine is functioning at its mysterious proper purr. When it is not, you do your best with home remedies; and when your expertise is not sufficient, you are not embarrassed to seek assistance from professional medical personnel.

When it comes to your child's flesh, you know your limits. Why do you feel humiliated when you reach your "wit's end" about his or her even more mysterious spirit?

Though your hearts *know* the unique way to bring your child to the fullness of life, there will be times when you are not in touch with your heart's infallible knowledge. Some days your thinking will cloud your inner wisdom. On these cloudy days the whole world fits into one big set of parentheses and you are unable to open yourself to a single thing.

The phenomenon of "closed-mindedness" results in days when your parental inner wisdom seems inoperative. Being out of touch with your deep intuitive parental sense is caused by being too close to the situation. Because of your emotional involvement, your own inner dynamics or those of your unique children are unclear. During these times, do not be embarrassed to seek some clarification from a detached third party. That third party can be a minister, a friend or a professional from one of the helping professions.

Much as a person viewing an automobile accident from the vantage point of a hill can see both sides of the story that will be given to the police, a detached third party can hear what both you and your children are saying. Once the emotional blockage that keeps you from being able to see the correct course of action is removed, you will once again be in touch with that unique wisdom that so infallibly guides you.

As the detached third party in many instances, I have often witnessed the dynamics of this process of emotional clearance. For example, a young girl, age 15, once came with her mother to see me about a problem that was emotionally separating them. They entered the room in an obvious, as well as painful, state of "cold war." The cause of the conflict was marijuana.

The very word *marijuana* was emotionally charged for the mother. The only information the mother had regarding the drug was gleaned from conversations with her friends, all of whom believed that marijuana was in itself addictive. Because of this "fact" the mother was unable to hear her daughter's insistence that she had only tried the drug twice and really did not like it at all. With the aid of some literature I happened to have on hand, the mother was able to see that marijuana, as such, was not addictive. The mother sighed in relief and was able to hear, for the first time, what her daughter had been saying. Shortly she and her daughter were able to hurdle the emotional impasse that had caused them to stumble in their communication. Both mother and daughter were able to embrace and shed a river of therapeutic tears.

Seeking help from a detached party is no more humiliating than when I ask someone to proofread what I have written. As many times as I go over a given page and correct *all* my mistakes, a proofreader inevitably sees something I missed. I am just *too close* to the pages before me.

There are times when my writing needs proofreading. There are times when your parenting needs some "objective" advice. These times do not make us failures, just human.

The Risk of Openness

It is important for parents, as it is for us all, to remember that no human being can be known in a closed way. This remembering will keep us all from missing who a person is because of whom we *expected* them to be.

Since no human being can be known in a static fashion, parents must be constantly opening their parentheses—and their ears—to their sons and daughters. This listening is a parent's full-time work.

Since your children are very unsure of their true "selves," they are easily overwhelmed by conventional thinking. You must be constantly inviting them to express their uniqueness.

Constant warning by alluding to standards outside of them and reminders of *your* expectations can make them hesitant about being themselves. Each time they do step out and test the waters of life by attempting to express themselves, they will take a giant step backward if they are faced with nothing but negative programming: "Be careful." "What will the neighbors think?" Or those deadly words that threaten their deepest instinctual need for security: "No child of mine will ever do such and such."

Not to encourage your children to express their "newness," their "one-and-only-ness," is to fumble your responsibility in the adolescents' most serious game of life.

If you are parenting with closed parentheses, you will know by a very painful sign—a sign written across your children's brow. The sign says: *I am prisoner. You are jailer.* Your adoles-

cents' feeling of being imprisoned by you has little to do with going out on Saturday nights, but much to do with going out on a limb to test their unique self-expression.

Allowing such latitude is much more difficult than closing parentheses on your children. Sometimes this openness is downright frightening. We all want to know what to expect in all of life's situations. But your children can never be the persons you expected them to be. They can only be the persons they are. You must give them room to grow, to become, to blossom.

Let me tell you about Rick, who helped me see the eternal value of keeping my parentheses open—even under intense classroom combat conditions.

Rick was a born comedian. If given the stage he was able, most of the time, to entertain easily and engrossingly for the better part of a class period. But it was a risky business letting "Rickness" loose. It was tempting to keep him contained.

Fortunately my subject matter made it possible for me even to allow Rick to upstage me on occasion. Sometimes I made errors in judgment. Sometimes I was too tired to restrain him when he was out of control of his very best self. Sometimes he went overboard. Some days he entertained perfectly. In the midst of the openness of this class situation, Rick had the opportunity to test himself, really to learn something of who he was.

As a junior and senior Rick won the leads in every school production. Later he returned to tell me that he was awarded the lead in a summer-stock road show. His words are still etched in my heart. "I gained all my confidence in your class, Father."

Parents also find it a risky business to let the uniqueness of their sons and daughters loose in the world. Parenting without parentheses demands that you approach every stepping-stone of your adolescent's life as you did his or her first baby steps—positively: "Come on, you can do it!" "Don't worry, I will catch you." "It's okay that you fell; try again."

Imagine how damaging it might have been for your infant to hear, "Don't try to walk, you might fall and embarrass yourself." Of course you felt nervous when you let go of those little hands. As much for your own comfort as your baby's, you rushed in to say, "Boom, boom!" when he or she fell. But you never lost your strength to keep encouraging your child until the day he or she walked *independently*.

Remember the feeling? The way you helped them on the physical level then should give you the hope that you will be able to do it again on the deeper levels of your adolescent's unique journey in life.

Your child will not stay inside a parenthetical prison; he or she cannot. Our very inner being struggles to *be*. This struggling to become our true self is not mere poetry but the perfectly made plan of a loving God.

If you want to help your child grow and become free, take the bars of your own thinking, your "idea" of your child, and bend these bars

open. When your children do step out they will not be without faults, rough edges, very real sin. Like Rick, their coming out will often be awkward. But, like Rick, I promise you they will be much more fun to have around the house.

It is very hard for parents, as it is for teachers, to remain open. Closed parentheses look so *right*. Each time we do bend the parentheses open, each time we refuse to imprison another human being, we are making an act of faith. We are saying, in effect, that we believe God made this person good. We will be rewarded by discovering this goodness firsthand if we have the ears to hear.

If you read the remainder of this book it is because you want to bend your parentheses into ears. With such "ears" you will be able to help your adolescents hear their own truth, and their truth will make them free. What better gift can you give them? What more can you offer these children God has invited into your living rooms and committed to your loving care?

Bending Isn't Easy

One warning is fair: Bending is never easy. May I suggest that you begin by meditating on the mother of Jesus. Imagine raising *that* adolescent. And though we do not know for certain, Mary may have had to raise Jesus without the help of her husband Joseph during some of the most crucial years in this child's unique life.

Imagine what happened to Mary's concept of "a good little Jewish boy" the day she saw him bantering with the learned rabbis in the Temple. Imagine the shock to her parentheses as she stood at the foot of the cross, her child of promise condemned as a common criminal.

As a faithful Israelite, Mary had certain expectations about what a Messiah would be like. These parenthetical ideas were thrown far out of kilter. Yet Mary never lost confidence in the goodness of her son. She went from the Temple to the cross and "treasured all these things and reflected on them in her heart" (Luke 2:19).

Mary managed. So will you.

In your son or daughter, God has given the world a priceless gift. Your work is to open the gift by attentive listening. Since you do not know what is in the package, you should have no preconceptions, no parentheses. All we know is that God gives only good gifts. So be prepared for a very pleasant surprise.

Heart-to-Heart Discussion Starters

1) What do you understand by the phrase "parenting without parentheses"? What do you *think* about the idea?

2) What are your *feelings* about "parenting without parentheses"? Comfortable? Disturbed?

3) What keeps a parent from parenting without parentheses?

4) Have you ever experienced being put into parentheses? By whom? How did this experience affect you?

5) Can you think of examples from your life when you were forced to open your parentheses, change your idea about a person, place, event?

Role Play

Choose two people, one to be the parent, the other the son or daughter. Roleplay this incident—and what might follow: You are sitting in the living room and your offspring accidentally drops a marijuana cigarette.

2. The Art of Adult Behavior

Recognizing the Adolescent in Ourselves

What is going on inside you and me? Obviously this question is very complex. To find out we have, more so in recent years, turned to the science of psychology. One psychological model or system that can give some insight into our complex inner dynamics is Transactional Analysis (TA). A familiarity with this approach can help us examine your role as a parent of an adolescent.

Perhaps you already know about TA. Many of us were introduced to it with the popularization of books like *I'm O.K., You're O.K.*, by Dr.

Thomas Harris. For those who are not familiar with TA, I'd like to introduce its vocabulary in a simplified form since these terms will be used as a focal point for the remainder of this book.

We all have within us three psychological "ego states":

1) *Parent:* This part of us represents the fixed messages we recorded in early childhood. These messages, called *tapes*, can be *critical* (negative)—for example, "Don't spill," "Don't touch," "That is bad"—or *nurturing* (positive)—for example, "Keep warm," "Keep trying."

2) *Child:* This part of us represents our responses to these early messages (tapes) which make us feel either affirmed or deprecated. For example, a child constantly reminded of physical delicacy may continue to underestimate his or her ability to do things in later adult life.

3) *Adult:* In this ego state one has the ability to listen maturely to the fixed messages of both *Parent* and *Child*, integrate the good advice and overcome the negative aspects, and with this information decide the best course of action in the here and now.

How It Works

These inner ego states struggle for control

over an individual. The struggle may be sparked, for instance, when you are unexpectedly asked to give a five-minute report to your club. If you are not accustomed to speaking before an audience, your *Parent* and your *Child* react simultaneously with tapes from the past.

Your *Parent* scolds, "Don't slouch!" (a negative tape), or encourages, "Assert yourself!" (a positive tape).

Your *Child* admits, "I'm scared!" (negative tape); then adds, "But it is exciting to be talking in front of all these people" (a positive tape).

Your *Adult* steps in to integrate the programming from the past with the present information:

"Yes, it is a good thing to watch my posture" (constructive use of the negative *Parent* tape).

"Yes, I do need to assert myself" (using the positive *Parent* tape).

"I will hold on to the podium for security" (awareness of the *Child's* fear).

"It is fun and flattering to be up here, so I'm going to enjoy it" (echoing the positive *Child* tape).

This process, of course, happens instantaneously. It is clinically dissected here only for the sake of clarity. It takes time and growth in maturity for us to recognize the ego state from which we are acting on our environment at a particular time.

The interaction between ego states grows more complex when two or more people are involved. In "transactions" with others, we can act as *Adult* to *Adult*, *Child* to *Child*, *Parent* to *Child*, *Parent* to *Parent*, *Adult* to *Child*, and so on. As the number of people increases, the combination of confusing ego states multiplies. In a simple family conversation, the combinations can be tremendously complex and can change rapidly.

Let us look at what happens at a family table when a teenage daughter announces she is pregnant.

The daughter has made an *Adult* decision: "I know I have made a mistake and acted irresponsibly, but now I need help." At the same time her *Parent* is scolding: "I feel so evil; I did the biggest *don't*." And her *Child* is shaking with fear: "My father is going to kill me!"

Her announcement sets up the same conflict in her parents, and each of them must quickly choose a response from among the promptings of *Parent*, *Child* and *Adult*.

If his *Parent* takes over, the father may say, "I told you to stay away from that boy," affirming his daughter's *Parent* tape. Mother may respond from her *Parent* tape to address the daughter's frightened *Child:* "That's all right, baby; you didn't mean to do it."

If the father's inner *Child* speaks, he may echo his childhood fear of being disliked: "What will the neighbors say?" Mother may respond with her *Child*'s uncontrolled ecstatic emotion: "Oh, I'm going to be a grandmother!" But neither parent's *Child* can provide constructive help to the daughter.

If both parents respond as *Adults*, the conversation may sound like this:

"Gee, honey, you must be living in terror.

How can I help you?" asks Father.

Mother adds, "We must get you to a doctor and see that you and the baby are all right."

It is clear from the above example how complex family inter-transactions can become. Each family member must integrate his or her inner tapes and respond as an *Adult* in the here and now. When father, mother and daughter all do the *Adult* thing, the best course of action will be taken. The daughter will still feel loved, even though the father may have to admit that his fear is so great and ingrained that he cannot bear the public scandal and wants his daughter to go away for a while. The mother might be able to say that even though she wants to "baby" her daughter, it is important for the daughter to accept responsibility for her actions. The daughter might feel very pleased with herself that she did not have an abortion, even though her great fear of "being killed" by her father had tempted her in that direction.

Until all three persons in the family make some *Adult* decisions, a great deal of what TA calls *cross-transactions* will be occurring. For example, confusions occur when a *Parent* ego state is talking to a *Child* ego state—particularly when both persons believe two *Adult* ego states are communicating.

Let's look at another example of cross-transaction by reviewing what happens when a friend tracks mud onto another friend's floor.

As inner *Parent*, Friend #1 says, "Hey, wipe your feet!" Friend #2, becoming a *Child* interiorly, reacts from an inner tape of childish reac-

27

tions and says something like, "Don't get uptight about a few specks of dirt! Hell, half the world is living in squalor and you are nit-picking over this."

When this transaction occurs, Friend #1 must apologize for treating an adult friend like a child. Friend #2 must apologize for the childish reaction. Analysis shows this transaction to have been *Parent* to *Child* and not *Adult* to *Adult*.

Straightening out the miscommunication is the first point of order. Once both parties see what has happened, they then can speak to each other as *Adults*.

The host might say, "What I meant to say was, 'Please don't track in any mud.' " It will then be clear to the guest that the words were meant as a *request* and not as a *command*.

Something that happened during the day may have caused the host to be a little "off" or "beside" herself. The simple words—"I'm sorry, it's been a bad day. Even a little mud is getting on my nerves"—put both friends back into an *Adult* communication. In effect, the host is saying, "I'm sorry I treated you like a kid," and the *Adult* to *Adult* ratio is reestablished.

This "clearing the air" emotionally allows the guest to react as *Adult* and friend, not like a hurt two-year-old. The friend can then help the host overcome the bad day with a sympathetic ear. Also the friend can help clean up the mud.

Putting the Adult in Control

Our work, and the work of your adolescents,

is to keep in touch with the ego state that is impelling us or them at a given moment. As time passes we gain more self-knowledge in this area. We learn from past experiences what triggers certain reactions in us. For example, an adult person might realize that when his mother visits, he reverts back to the *Child*. When his mother says, "You do not dress warmly enough," he wants to react like a grownup but is already reacting like a child *inside*.

If he *denies* his inner reaction, he will deal his mother a cruel blow. He might say, "Get off my back, all right?" This response, of course, pushes his mother deeper into her role as *Parent:* "Is that any way for you to talk to your mother?"

If he accepts the feeling inside, he can then act maturely. An *Adult* can react like this: "You know, Mom, I appreciate your concern and love,

but when you carry on like that I feel like a two-year-old. I've made a decision not to wear a scarf. But thanks for your concern; it means a lot to me." And a kiss on the cheek can pleasantly punctuate the exchange.

The mother will realize she was acting as *Parent*, although the term she may use is "being pushy" or "butting in," and will drop it. She also will realize that she, as a person, is not being rejected—only her suggestion.

Until we integrate our ego states and learn to act *Adult*ly, we are all in adolescence. Adolescence is that period of growth in self-awareness when we *begin* to recognize our inner ego states and *begin* to operate from an *Adult* ego state. Some psychologists have claimed that adolescence lasts well into middle age. Many adolescent periods last much longer.

This tendency in all of us to remain adolescent, to avoid the pain of integrating our ego states—that is, to become *Adult*—is the reason parents must be very careful. Parents must constantly monitor themselves as they parent their offspring.

You can only help your sons and daughters on *their* way to adulthood, to full integration, if your actions are *Adult*—or if you have the humility to know when they are not.

When you allow your inner *Child* to give a command, you have stopped parenting. Such commands make you your child's sparring partner, not his or her parent. Seldom will you come to actual blows, but you can throw some very damaging psychological punches.

If your inner *Child* does swing below the belt and you are obviously being psychologically unfair, admit it. For example: "You pig, I said clean up that room *before* you leave this house tonight." In this situation, your inner *Parent* must catch you—as your own mother or father did when you were young—and make you do the *Adult* thing: apologize.

You are not apologizing for insisting that the room be cleaned—and pronto. You are apologizing for the use of the term *pig.* You, your *Adult* self, do not really think of your adolescent as a pig.

By apologizing you are not giving in or up, you are *parenting properly.* All you are doing is issuing new orders from *Adult* headquarters. "Please get your room in order. I mean now." Since your adolescents are not really happy with the lazy *Child* within them, they are more likely to respond to this kind of reminder.

Here is an example of a transaction from my teaching experience that may be of some value:

One day I walked into a class of junior boys the day "after the night before." A friend had unexpectedly arrived, and he and I sat up most of the night talking and toasting our conversation. The next day I felt like the cartoon character who asked his wife: "Did you see the elephant that walked across my tongue?" I wanted to be any place on earth but in Room 102 with 40 16- and 17-year-olds.

Since in schools, however, the show must go on and understudies are hard to find, I walked "on stage" unprepared. After the opening prayer, while I fumbled for a rousing first play though the mental cobwebs covering my standard game plans, a student spoke. He spoke *without* my permission. I became righteous. Inside, of course, I knew that his foul play was directly caused by my delaying tactics.

I stepped toward the student and slapped him across the face. Along with the physical pain he experienced, he was of course embarrassed in front of his peers. The young man then stood up (*without* my permission), spoke again (*without* my permission) and announced that he intended to go to the main office and see the principal, with or without my permission. His reason: "You hit the wrong guy, Father. It wasn't me talking."

Like a Monday night instant replay I saw clearly that he was right. The culprit sat in the seat behind my victim. It was the first, and I'm pleased to say, the *only* time I ever slapped a student; I was inexperienced in this most startling of situations.

In an attempt to restore normalcy to the class I spoke calmly: "Sit down. You, young man, are going nowhere." His next phrase came out politely, "I will not sit down." And since I had gravitated to the door, he said, "Please step aside." My *Child* grabbed my inner microphone and shouted, "Don't let this upstart get away with this." My *Child* continued to bellow, "You'll never gain the respect of this class if you give in here."

My inner *Adult* said, "For heaven sakes, you are wrong. You hit a kid, first of all. Secondly, you hit the *wrong* one. Thirdly, you were up all night and are unprepared. You did not discipline; you humiliated another human being."

So what did I do? I prayed. Yes, I did. When all else seemed at a loss, I prayed. Look on it as a spiritual punt. Then my *Adult* took over and quelled my inner *Child.* And I took my inner *Adult's* advice: I apologized. I acted *Adult*ly.

Much to my surprise the student's reaction was anything but what I had expected. I had expected him to tell me to take my apology to the moon. He did not. He said simply and with a smile, "That's okay, Father, no problem." He sat down. Somehow my apologizing defused his anger. He was no longer a bleeding carcass in the midst of his gaping classmates.

After class about five of the students came up to my desk. I presumed that this small group was a belated lynching party. These students asked me what I thought they ought to do in a situation in which they felt they were acting like "babies." Perhaps there is no connection, but it was the first time anyone in that particular class asked me anything other than, "What's going to be on the exam?"

We usually blame the evil in us on the devil. But the devil need not bother with most of us. We make ourselves do it. The process is simple, though it causes most of the complexities in our lives. We allow our *Child* or *Parent* to oust our *Adult* personality in a situation. Without the *Adult* in control, we become a wild child and/or a domineering parent.

For example: Your son forgot to mail a pack-

age you wanted in the mail *today*. When he tells
you, your reaction might be, "I want to murder
that kid for his irresponsibility." (This is your
Child talking because you fear what someone
else will think of your tardiness.) Or, "That's it,
no more privileges for a month " (a rather strict
Parent stance). When your *Adult* operates you
will hear yourself saying: "Hey, John, how come
you forgot to mail the package? You know how
much it means to your grandmother to receive
her birthday gifts on time."

Virtue: Standing in the Middle

Let's take one more look at the integrating
process that takes place so swiftly in an adult
personality. An example: The inner *Child* looks
at a pie and says, "Eat a piece." The inner *Parent*
says, "You are gaining too much weight." The
Adult registers the need expressed by the *Child*
for something sweet *and* the "caution" of the
inner *Parent*. The *Adult* then makes a decision:
"I'll eat lightly at supper and later tonight treat
myself to a piece of pie by the fireplace."

To act adultly we need what the saintly theologian Thomas Aquinas called *virtue*.

The word *virtue* comes from the Latin word
for power. If you want real power—not just
power stemming from the principle, "Might
makes right"—you need virtue. A virtuous person rules by "virtue of the respect" we have for
him or her, not by regulations. Virtue, according
to Aquinas, "stands in the middle."

Standing in the middle does not mean mediocre. Standing in the middle means mature. Virtue, then, means the *Adult* stands in the middle, between our *Child* ego state and our *Parent* ego state, and monitors our actions and words.

As you witness your adolescents' inner struggles to act *Adult*ly, you have special moments to educate, to draw forth their greatest human potential. For you really to "hear" what is happening within your adolescents as they struggle to integrate the energy of their inner *Child* with the wisdom of their inner *Parent* in an *Adult* manner, you must have wide open parentheses. Open parentheses are like enormous ears—the bigger the better. Remember?

Heart-to-Heart Discussion Starters

1) Do you feel a parent loses children's respect if the parent apologizes for "too strict" discipline?

2) Do you as a parent have a hard time being *Adult* in your disciplinary actions? Are you tempted to listen to your inner *Child* and be too nurturing, that is, too soft? Do you ever take the strictest route because it is the path of least resistance? Discuss.

3) How did you feel, as a child, when you were unjustly disciplined by your parents?

4) Is there any person in your life who evokes the *Child* in you? The *Parent* in you? Explain with examples.

Role Play

Situation: Your son was supposed to fill the car with gas when he used it last night for a date. This morning as you left to pick up your carpool for work, you looked at the gas meter and it registered near empty. You were running late, and the only open gas station was on the far side of town. *Now* it is 6 p.m. and supper has begun.

1) Choose members of the group to play mother, father and teenage son.

2) Consciously dissect the incident from the *Child*, *Adult*, and *Parent* ego states. For example: Father consciously brings up the topic of the empty gas tank as his inner *Child*. Witness the response from the son and mother. Then switch to Father acting as *Parent* and as *Adult*.

3) Discuss and compare reactions.

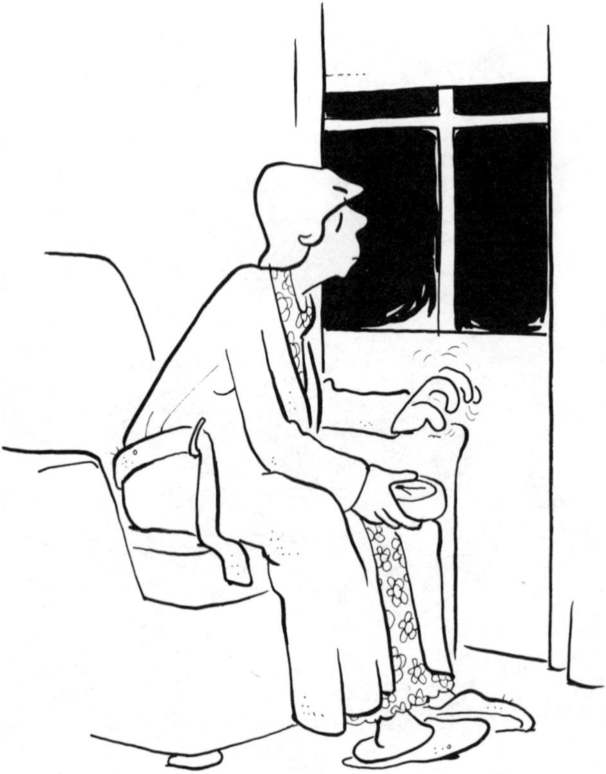

3. The Art of Losing Your Mind

P
is for Patience

Listening daily with big ears takes more patience, of course, than many of us have. Even when you are not exaggerating, it does seem that much of what you have to say to your teenagers is said for the *100th time.* An inherent quality of adolescence is being tuned into one's self and not into the selves of others. Therefore an adolescent is hearing the oft-repeated phrase *as if* for the first time. So until your adolescent does grow up, *you* need endless patience.

Unfortunately, Americans are running short of this crucial supernatural resource. We hardly have any patience, and few of have it in endless quantities.

Besides the internal struggle to become integrated, we have external pressures to challenge our patience threshold. McDonald-land has oozed through its plate-glass doors and under its golden arches into the sanctuaries of our homes. In spite of the blatant fact that millions of our dollars are passing over McDonald's counters each year, we cling to the belief that they "do it all for you"—and the "you" means *us*.

McDonald's slogan is extremely clever advertising. Unfortunately their ad keeps running subliminally in our heads. *For us.* Everything they are doing, they are doing *for us*. We know better. We know that without cash or coupon, McDonald's will do nothing for us—nor do we really expect them to. But the idea *"for us"* has sunk deep roots into our hearts. And, sadly, we have begun to apply the slogan to our families and friends. We have begun to expect them to be doing whatever they are doing *for us*. And fast.

When we are in our right minds—not *thinking*, but *knowing* what is the truth—we *know better*.

Yet an explosion can occur because a car is returned 10 minutes late. The explosion occurs because we thought the car *ought* to be home on time. That command comes from our rigid inner *Parent*. Or we decided we *wanted* the car home on time, because our inner *Child* had personal plans. So when it is not on time, we "fly off the handle."

Sometimes externals force us to be adult

before we force ourselves. The moment we hear the "facts" that our minds did not know, we must humbly backtrack. "Gee," says a nearly hysterical daughter, "I was held up by an accident and it turned out to be Mrs. O'Rourke. I think she's..."

In the meantime, that time before we are graced by God, we must suffer the embarrassment of being impatient. Remember, patience is a virtue. We often react to reality from our inner *Parent* or our inner *Child*. We often act like adolescents, not adults. Tremendous suffering results. The suffering is intense whether it is caused by the way we treat ourself or another. We want to be mature. We want to be flexible. We want to be loving toward others. We want, in short, what our adolescent offspring want: We want to grow up.

The inability to be mature is why your teenagers are in a perpetual state of inner commotion. The world allowed them to act like babies when they were small. Now the world around them is demanding they "grow up," "act their age." They are trying, but not very successfully. Despite the snug-fitting clothing they wear, nothing seems to fit in this junior-bizarre world. The result is suffering.

Your adolescent needs patience with himself or herself. So do you and I when faced daily with our own adolescent behavior. In high school you may have learned that the word *patience* comes from the Latin verb *patio*. *Patio* means to suffer. (If your Latin class was like mine, you learned the meaning of that word firsthand.) Our exposure to McDonaldese and all for which it stands has quickly programmed us to forget all we learned or must learn on the subject of suffering and patience.

Patience and suffering are necessary for our growth in maturity. Patience and suffering collaborate to keep us from merely becoming senile. A mature person has learned the art of patient suffering; a senile person merely exhibits extraordinary stamina.

Adolescence Means Suffering

During your adolescents' hurricane years, nothing is going their way. They are caught in the wake of childish irresponsibility, on the one hand, and overwhelming pressure from their inner *Parent* to "shape up," on the other. One day they will give in to the childish challenge: "I bet you can't drink the whole bottle." The next, they will be stricter with themselves than their real parents ever dreamed of being. The strictness comes from a very deep desire to be finished with the suffering of adolescence.

Adolescents vacillate between these two extremes. Adolescents have very little virtue, very little that stands in the middle. They rarely have the ability to stand on the pivotal point and see the adult thing to do.

Your children do not yet know their true selves. Until they do, there is intense suffering. During this "in between" time, the thing they need most is your encouragement. They need to see adults in action. Possibly you are only one step ahead in maturity, but with that lead you can show them the way. By your acceptance of your mistakes, your openness to change, your ever-mellowing spirit, you can effectively demonstrate adult behavior.

One mature action is worth a thousand words. Why? Because adolescents, like us all, see with inner eyes the *whole* picture. If you are adult in your actions, your adolescent will be encouraged to win the struggle waging in his or her own "insides."

The day an adolescent stops looking all over the place for his or her real self, he or she will begin to look in the right place—within. Until that day, he is like spilled milk all over the table; she is like an out-of-control vehicle—and certain brakes must be applied: namely, *external* discipline. But external discipline must be right.

Effective discipline takes into consideration the internal struggle raging between the *Parent* and *Child* ego states in the adolescent. Your son has been speeding. This means his inner *Child* has taken charge. A way to discipline might be: "Listen, John, we want you to use the car, but when you drive like you did yesterday, someone has to stop you. It is a matter of safety. Who will it be, you or us?"

Perhaps your child's inner *Parent* is the problem. Let's review this example: "We expect you to do well in school, too; but your father and I have noticed you are being too strict on yourself. Take some time off this weekend and relax."

Apply proper ointment to your adolescent's

inner wound: The result is healing.

By knowing where you personally need discipline, you will see where your adolescents need it. They may think you can read their minds, and in a sense you can, because you can read your own.

This period of adolescence is exhausting for your teenager. It is also exhausting for you. For you it sometimes seems like you are having a bad dream when your adolescent reverts to childish behavior patterns. But these emotionally stormy days are also like bad dreams—even nightmares—for your adolescents. They want to wake up. But until they can handle their *inner selves* and become integrated, the "how to" is in your hands. With the patience you have gained by your own suffering, you can patiently guide your children through their adolescence into maturity.

To discipline an adolescent properly one needs the patience of Job and the timing of a secretary of state. Therefore you, as disciplinarian, need prayer. Whatever else prayer means to you, it should mean one thing: A pray-er is a person who stands before the living God in his or her psychological birthday suit and pleads for aid.

It may bring you some consolation to hear that you are not alone in your struggle to be patient. You have a host of comrades suffering from the same inner tension. To me it is no surprise that as parents you find your patience tried. Nor is it shocking or difficult to understand why you are often guilty of "flying off the handle" with the slightest provocation. You, as a parent, are under enormous pressures. Pressures from without and from within. It is a wonder that you have *not* lost your minds. But, unfortunately, you haven't.

Suprised that I said "unfortunately?" Your surprise is natural enough, but *natural* is *not* enough if you intend to parent openly.

We all want to "keep" our minds, and the mind is a good thing to keep—in control. But that is not the usual way it works. Too often our *minds keep us*, *control us*, rather than being kept in control.

Let's look at an example. We have all had the experience of waiting—for a person to arrive, for a medical report, for a bus. If we were just waiting, there would be no problem. No anxiety. But then our mind takes over and causes us to worry: "I wonder what the doctor will find? Cancer? If he does find it, what will happen to the family?" The mind tortures us.

Waiting and Worrying

Parents wait for the return of a late child at night. "Whatever can be keeping that kid? I hope he is all right. It is so slippery outside." Worry. You are in a mental torture chamber.

What we must all learn is how to wait without worrying. It is a difficult lesson to grasp. It is a lesson we can only learn by grace. Until we do receive the grace to wait without letting our minds put us through hell, we must accept the accompanying suffering. And if it is any help, as was said about patience, we might remember we are not alone in our suffering.

Since our minds do control us and not vice versa, we are bound by our thinking. This is why we marvel at people who say they "don't mind" when set plans are altered. We say such a person is very polite. Actually, if the words are sincere, he or she is very holy. Such people are "out of their minds," open to reality as it is and not as they think it *should* be.

"Listen, Joan, I know you have been looking forward to your vacation for such a long time, but we need to get the inventory. . . . You don't mind? Really? Oh, Joan, you are great." Yes Joan is. A great saint or a great liar. It is no great virtue to say, "I don't mind," when we do mind terribly. It is a lie. A socially acceptable one, that is true, but let's not lose track of the fact that it is merely a way to save face. We want to look good. Polite. Be a nice person. It is all ego and proud.

But remember: Being ego-filled, full-time face-savers is our condition. It is not what we want, but it is who we are. It is the truth.

So we do live most of the time "minding" our business *a lot*. When Johnny comes strolling in at 12:30 instead of 11:30, you do *mind* very much. Your mind has tortured you. You are not a saint. Good, yes; perfect, no. Your thinking has practically driven you insane. The blithe words, "What's the big worry, such a big deal," do not sit well. Don't be surprised if you are *not* "polite"!

The dynamic of Johnny's return is simple.

Your teenager had his head full of facts. He knew his location. He knew he was safe. He knew he was not harming himself.

You had a mind full of fiction. You had imaginary thoughts. Had you had the facts—"*Why* didn't you call?"—the dynamic would be different.

You know the answer to your question. Johnny had no good reason to call and request an extension. He chose to "risk it." You are furious mainly because you have lived an hour of fear.

Perhaps you will never be able to change this pattern but, if you watch carefully, an opportunity will arise to teach your adolescent an important lesson. Be vigilant for a day when he or she is worried sick. She is waiting for the results of a big test. He is waiting for the answer from his auto insurance agent regarding his claim. When your children are sharing their anxiety, let them step into your shoes. Don't say, "What's the big deal?"—even if you are tempted to do so. Say instead, "I know that this is a very big problem for you and I want to tell you something that will help you understand your parents better."

Then proceed with an explanation something like this. "Do you know why you are worried? Because you do not know what is going to happen. Your worry is normal. You feel awful. Well, when you are out at night and don't come home at the agreed time, we feel the way you feel now. We don't know what is happening and so we worry. That is why we are so touchy when you come home late."

Your adolescent's worry provides a very educable moment. He or she can learn a great deal in a few short minutes. This does not mean curfew will never be broken again. All you can hope for, and it is a great deal, is that when it is broken your feelings will be better understood. You may even hear, "I know how worried you must have been but..." The excuse, valid or not, is really irrelevant; the lesson has been learned.

When your adolescents know what is going on inside of you, they may be less prone to misunderstand your words. "Where have you been?" becomes a question of love and not one of accusation. They now know that you are more concerned about the *you* in the question than about the *where*.

This does not mean you are not interested in their whereabouts. You are. But try not to be too interested. Adolescents, like you, need a certain amount of privacy. Sometimes they will keep their activities to themselves. They do so for no more devious reasons than when you kept your own parents guessing.

Experimenting Into Adulthood

Adolescence is an extremely experimental age. They are trying out various formulas for success with the opposite sex, for popularity with their peers. They are trying to announce the "good news" of their existence on this planet.

Their announcements sometimes come off badly because in their heart of hearts they do not really believe in their own self-worth. This is why they look so hard for signs of their worthwhileness. First they look to *you; then* their peers. They also look to teachers, to coaches, to anyone who affirms their goodness.

You are naturally disappointed when your son or daughter does something that risks your disapproval to please the peer group. But, remember, you did the same. The pressures to conform are great for the non-adult.

I can give you an example from my life which may help. It was the first time I drank too much alcohol. I was experimenting, and it blew up in my face.

Some older friends whose approval I needed smuggled me into a bar. We drank delightful-tasting concoctions called Seven-Sevens—and I had no idea how lethal they could be. I drank at least seven. When I stood up, I was at best able to crawl without help.

I was visiting my older brother and his family at the time. I felt he would be upset if I came home inebriated. Add in the fact that I was a seminarian and my desire not to give "bad example" weighed on my shoulders. The effort of controlling the weight of my body with a weightless brain and the heavy fear of encountering my brother before the effects wore off made me a full-time project for two of my comrades.

When I arrived at the front door, my worst fears were realized. My brother had decided to stay up and watch a late movie. So I sat down on the sofa, wound up my wobbly lips and threw my first verbal pitch—an attempted curve to distract. Here is how it went.

"Um, did the Sunday *Tribune* arrive yet?" I said slurringly.

"No," replied my brother.

"Oh," I said, "it usually comes by this time on Saturday."

My brother agreed, but informed me that it was Friday and, "Furthermore, you are drunk; go to bed."

The next morning my brother sent my nephew into my room to wake me up. I heard my brother laughing and saying, "Wake the drunken bum up." The laughter was music to my ears. Obviously my brother had not taken my experiment too seriously. He understood. He did not act as if I had stolen the crown jewels, nor did he award me the medal of honor. He took my mistake with a grain of salt and let my hangover be my just punishment.

Because of his understanding reaction, I remember being open to his advice. That same night I was going to a wedding reception, the reason for my visit with my brother. He knew that at the reception minors and alcohol would be mixing. So my brother left me with these words of advice: "Remember how you felt this morning. So be careful tonight." I remembered. And I was.

Our experimenting with life continues until adolescence is completed. A person who is an adult *knows* how much to drink. An adolescent *thinks* he or she knows. There is a difference.

When we say we *think*, it means we do not really *know*. "I think I did well on the exam" is not the same as "I know I did very well." Adolescence is therefore a tremendous period of thinking. Adolescents and adolescent adults know very little.

If you can remember that adolescence is an experimental stage, you will treat your offspring the same way you would treat a cancer research scientist. You would not go into a laboratory and demand that the researcher know an answer to the problem of cancer. You would ask, "How is your research going?" "What have you learned?" "Do you have any theories?"

This exploratory approach will help your adolescent in his or her research program to figure out the complexities of life. "You experimented with drinking. Okay, what have you learned?" You then can bring in your life "notes" and compare.

This approach takes infinite patience. It takes a radical bending of your parentheses. It is difficult. But by looking at *your* insides first, you may be better able to accept the challenge of parenting without parentheses.

Charity does begin at home. If you are at home with yourself, at home with your insides, you will find the insides of others acceptable. If you can let your adolescent's insides show comfortably in front of you, your house will become a home. Parents without the patience to be open to their children often find their homes have become mere check-in stations.

On days when it seems you may not make it,

read the following words by St. Paul. Paul was one of the most mature men ever to be called Christian, but he had to struggle with *his* insides too: "I know that no good dwells in me, that is, in my flesh; the desire to do right is there but not the power. What happens is that I do, not the good I will to do, but the evil I do not intend" (Romans 7:18-19).

We can easily translate Paul's words into the terminology of TA. Paul's *flesh* means the struggle between his inner *Child* and his inner *Parent*, while he has a real, true self that wants to do the *Adult* thing. But Paul says he has no power. In many situations he has no middle or mature way. He has no virtue. So he ends up doing the evil he does not want to do. Perhaps he found himself "flying off the handle" with the Christians of Corinth, Rome, Galatia.

Eventually, we know, Paul became an adult. That is why we call him "Saint." He became integrated. His adult self won the crown. Paul lived to tell the tale; so will you. Let your heart lead the way. If you do, you will hear your heart telling you, "Go in peace, your faith has saved you."

Heart-to-Heart Discussion Starters

1) What are some typical situations in which you find your self "flying off the handle" with your teenagers?

2) Analyze the situation mentioned. Why do you get upset? Are you *Adult* in your reaction?

3) Do you feel the "instant" mania to which we are exposed (e.g., the fast food phenomenon, instant print, quick marts) is making us prone to be less patient than our own parents?

4) In what kinds of situations do you find you have "infinite" patience? What is the inner dynamic in these situations?

Role Play

You just received a telephone call from your mother-in-law. She has been waiting at the doctor's office for your son to pick her up. He is now one hour late. Seconds after she calls, he wanders in lackadaisically. You ask why. He announces he "forgot." React.

1) Roleplay the situation giving your honest reactions. Have the group analyze the inner dynamic.

2) Roleplay again, acting upon different ego states in yourself.

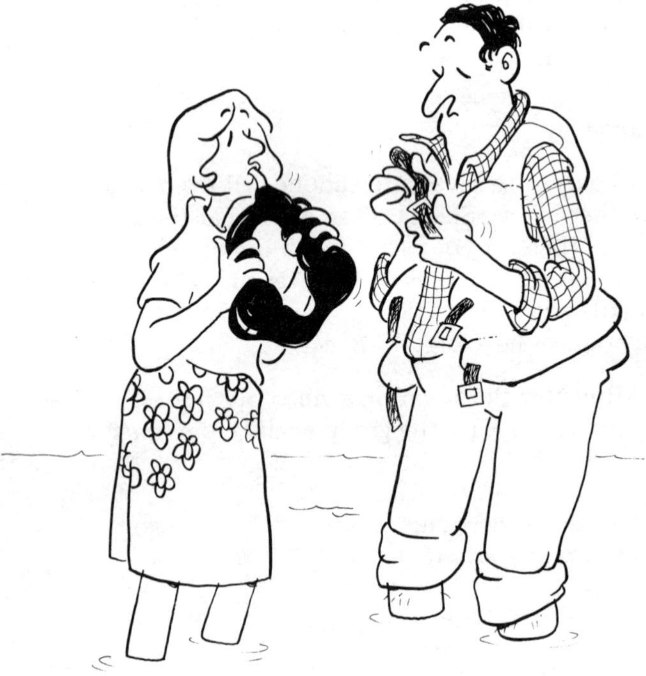

4. The Art of Affirming Your Adolescent

A is for Anger

A child, like a river, *can* rise above its source. But a river swelling beyond the embrace of its banks means flood. And floods are most disturbing.

A classic example of a child stretching beyond the bounds of his parents' thinking is St. Francis of Assisi. Francis' name has become synonymous with the ideal of poverty, yet his father, until his dying day, remained wholly committed to his wealth.

Francis Bernardone rose above the confines of his environment, the confines of his father's parentheses; so can your children. But that "flood" means tremendous anguish and anger. Pietro Bernardone thought Francis mad, and this "madness" only further infuriated him.

Better for you and your adolescent if you can avoid floods by rising with the tide and keeping in touch with the ebb and flow of your adolescents' unique moments on this earth. But that takes a tremendous ability to respond (response-ability) and a profound courage to let your sons or daughters be whoever they will be.

To get some idea of how frightening this process of allowing emergence in your very own teenager can be, let us look at a teenager with whom you are not so emotionally involved. His name is Simeon. Simeon is a real person from the pages of history, even though his life sounds like the product of someone's imagination gone wild.

At the age of 15, Simeon asked an old man in his parish how best he might please God. The wise old man spoke eloquently of the Beatitudes, of fasting and prayer. Simeon's heart burned. He entered the local monastery, but after a few years of extraordinary penances Simeon was dismissed from the monastery as "a bit strange."

As if to prove the abbot's point, Simeon did something which made the hunchback of Notre Dame seem like an average swinging bachelor by comparison. Simeon built himself an 80-foot-high tower. On top was an unsheltered platform a few feet square. He climbed to the top, perched himself and remained there for 37 years.

Try to imagine how you would feel if this were *your* son. How would you feel when his remarkable behavior began drawing comment from the neighbors: "Did you see what their son, Simeon, is up to?"

Simeon's bizarre behavior was eventually considered holy by the Church. Now he is *Saint* Simeon. He lived to see thousands imitate his asceticism. Scores begged his advice and prayers.

But what of his poor parents? Before the rave reviews came in, Simeon's parents had to judge *for themselves*. They were simple shepherds and not as "heady" as we have almost been forced to become. They had the heart to know that their ways and God's need not necessarily coincide. They had the faith to know that their son was doing the correct thing—for him—even if everyone else thought differently. This is not permissiveness, but piety. And, for this reason, almost all the lives of the saints begin the same way: "St. So-and-so was born of pious parents..."

Probably your children will not desire to sit atop a pole. When they begin to uncover their true identity, however, they may wish to go *out on a limb*. When they do, where will you be? That depends on whether you see the world through the eyes of Emily Post or the eyes of God. In the first case, you will be trying to pull them back to "safety"; in the second, you will be under the branch ready to catch them if they fall.

Your responsibility is to encourage your children to discover their deepest "within." Authentic encouragement helps your child find the unique meaning of his or her particular life. Authentic encouragement demands that you not insist that their "within" fit within *your* "within." You must work daily to overcome the temptation to confine your sons and daughters within your own parentheses. Your challenge is to help your children grow into the image and likeness of their *creator*, not their *parents*.

Why Adolescents Get Angry

All of us are greatly influenced by the society in which we live. All societies do a lot of confining of individuals. This social pressure to conform is experienced in a particularly acute way by adolescents.

Because adolescents have a strong need to fit into the expectations of others, they try to bend their uniqueness in order to be acceptable. The bending does not work. Anger results. This is why your adolescent flies into unpredictable rages.

This anger is not bad. It is good. It is a sign of life. The anger means that when the bending does stop, an exciting human being will emerge. Until the emergence, however, it is painful for both you and for your son or daughter.

Unfortunately you are often the recipient of your offspring's pent-up anger. Dealing with that anger is a real challenge for most parents.

When your teenagers fly into an angry rage, you only aggravate the situation by asking them, "What's the matter?" They do not really understand what is wrong with them.

Asking this question is much like asking a lost child in a crowded department store, "Where is your mother?" That question only makes the child cry harder because his mother's absence is *the problem.* The proper kind of question can help calm the lost child. For example, "Do you want me to help you find your mother?" or, "Do you want us to call your mother over the microphone?" Likewise, the proper question may help your teenager resolve his or her feelings of hostility.

To know the *right* question will demand that you be a good listener—that you be attentive to what the real cause of the anger might be.

Adolescents' anger usually results from some incident in which they have stifled their own uniqueness. At some moment during the day they may have heard their true self, but failed to respond authentically. That failure is eating away at them and causing them to be angry.

You can help them discover the root of their anger by helping them search their day for some clue to the feelings they now have. You might ask, "Did something happen at school today that made you feel bad?"

If the answer comes back haltingly, "I'm not sure," then pursue. They are embarrassed to admit their weakness, even to themselves.

You might entice them to be honest with themselves by sharing from your own experiences of failure. You might say, "I can remember from my high school days how I sometimes went along with the crowd and was pressured to cheat." You have to go fishing for clues, and your adolescent's face will tell you when you have a nibble.

As you continue you may hear, "You know, something did happen today. . ." (You are over a big hurdle; now you only have to listen carefully.) "Everyone was pushing that new kid around and he dropped his books all over the place. His notebook broke open and papers flew everywhere. Well, I went to help, but I saw some of the guys look at me. . . Well, I just walked away."

Now you can help again. You can assure your child that he is okay even when he isn't his best self. He needs to know that you know he is perfectly lovable, even if he is not perfect.

Before you can ask the right questions or be of any help to your adolescent, you must know what is going on inside of you. If your inner *Child* is too angry to help your adolescent, take your inner *Child* out for a walk. Kick a few trees. When you are your *Adult* self again, return and attempt to guide your son or daughter. Adolescents dead-ended by the swirling maze of questions in their head need a parent, not another person in a pout.

Parents also need to understand the various kinds of anger. Unlike anger in a child or an adult, adolescent anger is caused by something within.

A child's anger is non-reflective. A child is not angry at his or her own weakness, but at the environment. A child wants to play with the television dials; his or her parent says *no*. Anger results because the child was "crossed." A child reacts to external stimuli.

An adult also becomes angry because of something outside. Adult anger is caused by seeing something that is keeping human beings from being their very best selves. For example, the institution of slavery incenses an adult. So does segregation—and war. An adult does not react *to* external stimuli but acts *upon* them—constructively. Adult anger tries to change the cause for anger.

Adolescents get angry at themselves. They are furious at their inability to act adultly, in an integrated manner. This inability causes them anguish.

A child's anger ceases when the child gets his or her way. Adult anger abates when *the* way, the truth seen through the eyes of God, is accepted by others. Adolescent anger stops only when teens can forgive themselves for not being perfect.

For adolescents to forgive themselves they usually need some help from an adult. That's where parents can come to their rescue and help them do the adult thing—that is, forgive themselves for being merely human.

Believing in Your Adolescent

Adolescents, as long as they are adolescents, are in an emotional purgatory. Their redemption can be heralded by your reminders that they are all right as they are. You can, in effect, save them from living a life "in hell." This means, of course, that you must really believe in your own heart that it is okay for a human being to be *just* a human being.

Adolescents can indulge in baby tantrums. So, as we know all too well, can we. They find it difficult to express their anger adultly. So do we. Adolescents *want* to express their anger in an adult manner. This "wanting to" is the driving force that makes them "madder than hell" each time they express their irrepressible and painfully unexplainable adolescent anger. With responsible direction from you, that little pressure-cooker about to explode will one day be a remarkable human being. Then you will not care what the neighbors have to say!

Of course that authentic self emerging in your adolescent may not be socially acceptable. Jesus' authentic self was very unacceptable to his contemporaries. But if they do *not* express that self, acceptable or not, they will *flip their lids.*

This doesn't necessarily mean they will end up in a mental institution. "Flip" behavior more frequently leads to taking refuge in a bottle, or work, or drugs. Most mental patients are walking the streets. (We need but consult our family physician to see how many *mental* patients he has.)

Your sons' and daughters' best health insurance is the assurance that you trust in their unique emergence. If you convey this trust, you will be able to heal some of the wounds they have already incurred on the battleground of daily existence. To be *this* trusting, to have your parentheses this open, demands faith.

Faith, we have heard, is a gift. Faith is not just a gift for *our* salvation. Faith is a gift we receive so we can release others from their personal "hells."

Adolescents go through hell until they learn to accept themselves as they are—both the good and the bad, the strengths and the weaknesses. Until they learn that being adult is a matter of a lot of grays, rather than blacks and whites, you can assure them that they are okay. Your eyes, your words, your arms can bring them to life at those times when they feel so dead, so foolish.

I recall talking to a woman who had a buried secret—a secret that was gnawing at her heart for 20 years. She had done a stupid thing. She had acted like a baby. One day in a rage at the humdrum of housecleaning, she had thrown a tantrum and ignited her house. It burned to the ground. Temporarily insane? Yes. She did not act adultly.

The moment she stood outside and watched the blaze, she knew "better." But then each lie—"The grease leapt up on the wallpaper!"—dug her true self in deeper. Her self-concept became as crumbled as the burnt-out rubble before her.

A psychiatrist was not necessary. She already knew her action had been insane. She was sorry. But who might she tell? Her husband? How could she? He had so sympathized with her suffering. Her friends? They had all rallied in a time of crisis. She was unable to share this dark secret with anyone. She kept the secret in her heart for almost a quarter of a century.

This agonized woman came to me in hopes of

releasing herself from her feelings of guilt. I assured her that she was okay. I pointed to the rest of her life—her daily struggle to be a loving wife and mother, the hours she spent giving, giving, giving. Slowly she began to see the whole picture.

She had not seen the whole picture all these years as she concentrated on a single frame: the day of the fire. So she had been living with a mistake, a childish act.

Finally the dam broke. She cried for 20 minutes. Then silence. Her lips quivered, then gently smiled. I knew from her expression she had just forgiven herself. She once again believed in her goodness. By the glowing expression on her face, I knew that I had just witnessed God's grace work through me as his instrument. I had committed an act of faith.

Becoming a 'Lie Detector'

No matter how successful we become in the eyes of the world, we will die angry if we die someone other than the unique person we are. In fact, we are already dead if we live an imitation of our true self.

Your teenager may be conned into thinking that he or she can "come alive" by downing a bottle of Pepsi. You know this is just not so. Sometimes you, when adolescent, think you can get more out of life from a bottle of Scotch. You know this also isn't so. The only way we come alive is to die to anything that is not authentically us.

You, unfortunately, must be the "lie detectors" for your adolescents. I say "unfortunately" because each time you call them for not being themselves, they will lash out at you. They will feel you are pushing too hard. But keep courage. One day they will look upon you as a life-saver. As long as you are acting from a response-able space within yourself, you are on the right track.

Many of us squirm when we hear Muhammed Ali expound, "I'm the greatest." Our squirming is a lack of faith that God really did make each human person the very best. Ali *is* the greatest. So are *you*. So are your sons and daughters.

Can you imagine God speaking in comparatives: "John is better than Joe"? Of course not. God speaks in superlatives. Only we, because of our lack of overall perspective, dare compare one human being with another.

There is a very sad slogan popular in current teenage retreat programs. The slogan expresses a real truth; it's just sad to realize that teenagers need such a saying to remind them of what ought to be an unforgettable fact: "God does not make junk."

Of course God doesn't. But *we* can. We can junk another human being because he or she does not fit into our parentheses.

Your sons and daughters, beautiful human beings, have forgotten the message that they are the greatest. They may not have ever heard it. You, by stepping into their corner, coaching them with your heart, can help them fight for, win and retain this God-given title.

Heart-to-Heart Discussion Starters

1) Do you think people tend to conform to an external or internal "blueprint" when they speak or act? Why?

2) Do you feel comfortable sharing stories of your weaknesses with your adolescents? Why?

3) Do you readily share your feelings with your children?

4) Do you agree that overwork, drinking too much, excessive TV watching are all signs of being uncomfortable with one's self? Explain.

5) Do you remember any incident in which you felt relief from guilt by telling a friend a secret? What caused the relief?

6) If someone tells you of a personal weakness, do you think less of that person?

7) Give examples of outbreaks of "adolescent" anger in your own life. How is facing the truth, accepting ourselves and learning to forgive ourselves the best antidote to this "adolescent" anger?

Role Play

Your adolescent just told you to "go to hell and stop your nagging." She then slammed shut the bedroom door. You turn the knob of the door and enter.

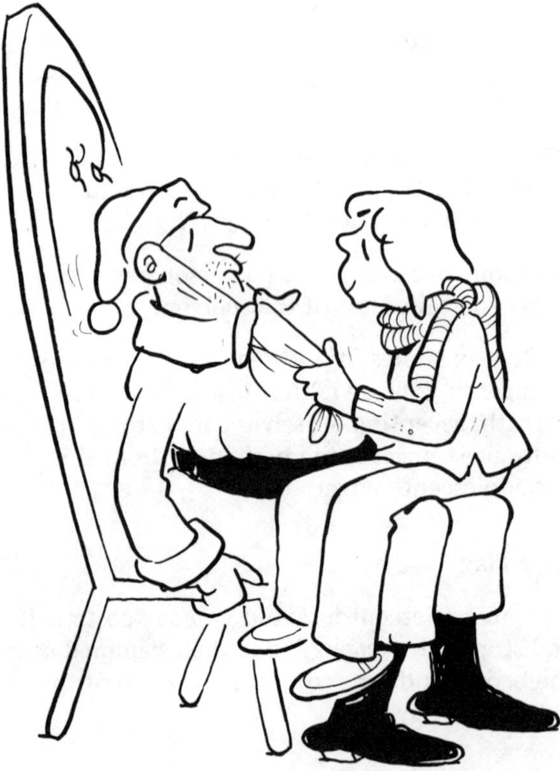

5. The Art of Believing

R
is for Religion

Adolescents are non-believers. As children, your sons and daughters believed in everything from Santa Claus to Sesame Street. Now that they are growing up and have technically become rational animals, they are no longer believers, strictly speaking. When they do become adult, they can become believers once again.

A real believer is a person who "puts his money where his mouth is." When we stop and look at our "mouthings" about the gospel and then review our lives, the reality of our own belief becomes suspect.

We say we wish to live as Jesus lived. Jesus lived simply. He lived ungraspingly, like the birds of the air. Yet we do not put our money where our mouthings are, but rather in banks, in investments, in down payments for "bigger and better" everything.

We are spiritual schizophrenics; we say one thing and do another. This is a clear way to describe what I will be referring to in this chapter as adolescent belief.

Adolescent faith is nothing more than the espousal of acceptable and *understandable* intellectual concepts. An adolescent "believes" what can be proven. But anything that can be proven cannot, once proved, be believed—no more than a book, once read, can be read for the first time.

An adolescent's faith is in the *reasonable.* But the last thing an act of Christian faith is, is reasonable. It is hardly reasonable to accept an infinite God become man. Faith, considered rationally, makes no sense.

Adolescent faith, then, is merely a collection of ideas *about* God that seem reasonable. So when your sons or daughters appear to be "losing their faith," you should be grateful, not disturbed. What this really means is that they are beginning to be distrustful of their "ideas" about God. This is good. Since God cannot be known only in our heads, cannot be contained by our ideas, your adolescents' doubts herald the possible beginning of an adult faith.

You were not upset the day your small child first questioned the existence of that "little old man with a red suit." You were able to use his or her doubt as a stepping stone to a more mature understanding of Christmas. The same holds true for your adolescent during this period of religious upheaval.

Many adults, with the spiritual transition begun by the Second Vatican Council, experienced the same confusion and doubt they now witness in their own adolescent offspring. If you experienced this inner conflict of clashing ideas and the resulting insecurity ("You mean the Church was wrong?") and even anger ("You mean my mother might have gone to hell for eating meat on Friday and I can eat all the meat I want?"), you will know the suffering of your adolescents. They too experience feelings of insecurity and anger when they discover that an idea that was once "true" is now in the category of "take it or leave it."

To illustrate the way an adolescent sometimes fights back, let me tell you of a small country parish and what happened when "communion in the hand" was first introduced. The vast majority of the parish accepted the change as natural and with an "it's about time" attitude. The "hold-out" was the teenage population. Many of them refused to consider opening their hands for Communion. Why? Being wise guys? Show-offs? Not at all. They were merely clinging to an idea.

So it is not only good and normal, but hopeful that your adolescents raise religious doubts. It is a sign of growth the day their religious "facts" become shaky. If they are shaken deeply the ground might become firm enough for God to step into their young lives. As long as your adolescents' heads are filled with answers, they cannot get to the Answer himself.

Only God has all the answers. We just have questions that cannot be satisfactorily answered this side of heaven. Adam was being very adolescent the day he gambled paradise by eating from a tree that promised the power to know all things. Adam wanted to be like God. So do adolescents. They want to know the *reason* for everything, and an adolescent never tires of the frequently irritating word *why*.

This is why the wonderful world of belief, including life's daily dose of "miracles," is beyond the scope of the adolescent who is trapped in his or her mind.

Being Born Again

Psychological adults know that they know nothing. They know their ideas are subject to change. They know that their knowledge is merely a very shaky collection of thoughts.

This sense of not knowing is the beginning of faith. Adults begin to "see" and "hear" with their hearts. On this day human beings begin the process referred to by Jesus as "being born again."

Being born again is like leaving the dark womb of the mind and seeing reality as it is and not as we *think* it is. This "first time" experience often makes the adult shout for joy and exclaim, "Now I see the light!"

Because the Kingdom of God is in our midst

if we have but eyes to see, Jesus insisted each must be born again to enter it. Jesus also insists that we become like small children if we wish to enter the Kingdom of God. Jesus is asking us to have faith like children. He is asking us to become real believers and abandon our adolescent faith.

Adult believers, like children, are not convenient. They bother us immensely. They are constant reminders of our own adolescent faith. It is humiliating to have them around. We become internally angry when someone witnesses to our own non-belief.

To overcome this anger at the belief of another, we need humility. Humility is a virtue. And we need that power to the *nth* degree. Humility simply means facing the truth. The truth is that many of us are stuck in our heads when it comes to our ability to believe, and because we take ourselves so seriously we do not have the humility to admit our lack of faith.

It is all right to be a non-believer. Really it is. This shouldn't be our ultimate goal in life, but it is all right if that is the place we are right now. By humbly accepting our lack of faith we will know the feeling of being saved even though we are just as weak and sinful and fumbling as ever.

This feeling of being saved is the experience handicapped persons have the day they really decide—in their hearts, not just in their heads—to accept their handicap. The missing limb does not reappear, but it is no longer a ghost haunting them day and night. Now they can get on fearlessly with the business of living.

The handicap of adolescent believers is over-reliance on intellect. Though our school report cards may not have shown it, we have all grown up too smart for our own good. We *think about* life more than we *live* it. We have all heard the saying, "Life is not a problem to be solved but a mystery to be lived." Yet we insist on knowing what life is all about.

Adolescents Need Reasons

Adolescent faith often leads to argumentation. Real faith, adult faith, leads to action. If I *believe* that the room in which I am currently sitting has a bomb that will explode in five seconds, I will not linger there. But if I only "believe" in my head—*think* there might be a bomb—I may just sit here because all my thoughts are debatable. I may be literally unmoved by my faith—unless, of course, there *is* a bomb.

Thinking does not make us *do* anything. Overweight people can think all day that they are slim—and nothing happens. As long as a person's faith is in the thinking stage, his or her faith is adolescent; nothing really happens. We are like slaveowners who "believe" all men are created equal.

Because of the scarcity of adult believers, G. K. Chesterton quipped, "The Christian ideal. . .has not been tried and found wanting; it has been found difficult and left untried."

Since adolescents' actions do not flow from their inner convictions, their real faith, they need a *reason* to do anything. And since adolescence is a period of self-concentration, self-centeredness, they need a reason that appeals to the self.

To the embarrassment of adolescents, the reason given must be in some way beneficial *to them*. They desperately wish this were not so. They so want to love, to give, to help simply for the sake of others. They cannot.

This inability is humiliating for an adolescent. But the first step to becoming mature and altruistic in their actions is acceptance of this humbling fact: Adolescents will do anything within reason *if* there is something in it for them.

As parents you can lessen your burden by presenting a selfish reason to your adolescent for an activity you see as necessary. "I've noticed, John, that since you have been taking out the garbage, you're getting better muscle tone." Manipulation? Yes. Good? No more than a pair of crutches are good. But crutches are helpful to a person who cannot walk without them. Reasons that make sense to an adolescent are necessary. Few adolescents can be counted on to do good deeds without some promise of reward. Those that can are adolescent only chronologically.

To give "good" reasons, ones that appeal to adolescents' needs for approval, demands an *Adult* parent. When you cannot think of a good reason, you are forced to use "*the* reason": "Because I said so, that is why!"

Before using "*the* reason" a parent must be very careful to evaluate honestly his or her inner dynamic. Who is issuing this order? Perhaps it is your exasperated inner *Parent* who is tired of listing reasons why. Perhaps it is your inner *Child* who wants your adolescent to do something because of a personal goal.

For example, your inner *Child* may really want to go on a long-planned fishing trip. Your son's recently announced desire to use the spare car for a big dance that same weekend may be clouding the issue. If you discern this inner dynamic and realize that your *Adult* self is "off duty," retreat in order to regroup your thoughts.

"*The* reason" ought to be used only rarely—and then only by a parent looking at reality from an *Adult* standpoint. If "*the* reason" is used too often or only when you are angry or exasperated, it will lose its effectiveness. Since "*the* reason" is an important weapon against the immaturity of your adolescent *when all else fails*, it is to be used wisely. Wisely means you are using "*the* reason" for *their*, and not *your*, sake.

The Sunday Mass Question

Since many of us are still very adolescent in many of our activities, we must humbly admit our own need for selfish reasons to make us do the right or good thing. This admission even applies to one of the best things we do each week: attending Mass.

If we were really adult, no reasons for attending Mass would be necessary and none could be given to keep us away. Adult believers want to go to Mass the way adult lovers want to be in each other's presence. The reason? Authentic love for the other, as other.

Few of us attend Mass because of a completely selfless love of God. Most of us still need a selfish reason for attendance. This is just the truth—and remember it takes humility to live our lives truthfully. And also remember it is all right to be just a weak human being.

The first category of reasons that moves our adolescent selves to attend Mass is "hard sell." The "hard sell" is commonly referred to as "fear of hell." The less offensive phrasing is "the Sunday obligation." It is embarrassing to admit that frequently, especially after an exhausting week's work, this approach is the only one that motivates us to kick our inner *Child* out of the comfort of a warm bed on Sunday mornings.

Another approach, one that appeals to the even-steven mentality of our adolescent selves, may be called the "Wall-Street approach." This is a way of keeping our heavenly stocks in order. We give time at work so we can collect our paycheck. We give time to our family so we can cash in on needed affection. So it just makes good business sense—it is very reasonable—to give time to God. When we die we will then receive our proper dividends.

Another approach, developed since the use of the vernacular and of modern music, may be called the "art of holy hustling."

The "art of holy hustling" is just the latest way of making attendance at Mass reasonable. Mass will be *enjoyable*—good music, good fellowship, and juice and donuts afterwards! A promise of pleasure always appeals to the adolescent.

Let us remind ourselves here of a crucial fact. These appeals to our selfish selves are not bad. These approaches are merely crutches. In fact, they are clever ways of getting us to do what our very best self, our adult self, really wants to do. They are ways to make the medicine go down until we know, not just think, that Mass is not only good for us, but good in itself.

In the meantime we must live with the humiliation of needing a reason. Oftentimes when the "hard sell" and the "Wall Street approach" fail, "holy hustling" motivates us to do the thing we want deeply to do: attend Mass. To the extent that we resist full maturation and get stuck in adolescent belief, more and more reasons will have to be given to us to attend Mass.

It is all right to need reasons as long as we are

admitting that we are adolescent. But to insist that the reasons make the Mass valuable is definitely putting the carriage before the horse. The Mass is valuable in itself. An adult knows that. This is why an adult goes to Mass *on principle* ("God is good and deserves our worship"), not *for a reason*.

The saints went to Mass on principle and for no reason at all. The saints were adult. They had character. The best definition of character I know is this: acting on principles from within, not from circumstances (reasons) from without.

It makes perfect sense to say a Mass was great because of the fabulous music and the great talk by Father So-and-so, but it does not make *infinite* sense. The circumstances do not make the Mass—except to *us* adolescents and to our *adolescent children*.

Therefore, until your adolescents do become adult, they will need reasons to attend Mass. When all else fails, you might hear yourself saying on Sunday morning: "Because I said so."

Someday, when they no longer live in your house, your sons and daughters will have to decide if they have any reason to attend Mass. Until that day you have the right and loving obligation to call them forth from childish "I don't wannas" ("I don't wanna go to school"; "I don't wanna take out the garbage"; "I don't wanna go to Mass") and from adolescent unacceptance of any reasons you can give.

You must call them beyond the pull of their inner *Child* by the strength of your inner *Adult*. You must pull until they show evidence that they are willing to push themselves or until it is out of your hands because they have moved out of your jurisdiction physically or by virtue of chronological age.

Once they do move into their own apartment, they will see reasons for taking out their garbage—even if it takes an odorous clout to their noses to discipline their inner *Child*. They will also, as they begin to move from adolescence into adulthood, find reasons for giving God his rightful worship. Life has a way of teaching us all that we cannot make it without keeping in communication with God.

Longing for God

Each of us wants to commune with God because God made us with a deep longing for him. This longing is so strong nothing on this earth can satisfy it. Nothing except God. None of the tinsel that tantalizes us for various periods of our lives—money, success, fame—can tame our restless hearts. All we want is God. God put that need in us. Some of us take a long time to figure it out. Others, like young Therese of Lisieux, understand this most unreasonable phenomenon at the tender age of 15.

Eventually we all learn that nothing except *Nothing* can fill us. *Nothing* with a capital *N* is God. He is *no thing* that we can possess, *no thing* we can think of—only God. Only a God who is *nothing* that has even entered the confines of our wildest and broadest imaginings can make us truly happy.

Your adolescent and your own adolescent self want the same thing: God and happiness. As a person ages, this desire for God and the happiness that he gives is the only reason that motivates us in our spiritual life. The times we read the Bible, go to church, live prayerfully are times we are sincerely seeking union with God. Any other reasons—Father's sermons, the opinion of neighbors who expect us to be churchgoers—will not motivate us. Only the pull of God, that supreme adult who sees beyond our adolescent and childish reluctance to be our very best self, can draw us to him.

When you do become adults and have virtue, you will become very power-filled parents. You will see the Spirit of God in your lives and will begin to trust, not in words alone, but in his power—the *only* power in heaven and on earth. On that day, the day you are no longer adolescent believers, your faith will be the size of a mustard seed—small, weak, feeble. But because it is *real*, you will be able to move the mountains of conflict that arise in your family. You will find in this religion of the heart the strength to bind you and your children together in an indestructible love, one for the other.

Heart-to-Heart Discussion Starters

1) Do you find it difficult to keep your parentheses open to your children's religious ideas? Why? Cite examples if you can.

2) Are there any "ideas" that you have been taught about religion that you are unsure of? Give examples. Discuss with group.

3) How would you react if your son or daughter came home and announced an interest in joining the Hari Krishna Society or following some swami, guru or yogi? What fears and feelings does such a suggestion arouse in you?

4) Have you ever doubted the existence of God?

5) Why, in light of what has been said in this chapter, is it impossible to prove to another that God does exist?

Role Play

You believe in an afterlife. It is your goal. You believe that when the time comes you will not fear death.

Now you have just entered the doctor's office and he has informed you that the tests have come back positive. You have cancer. He says, "There is a great deal of research being done, but as of now, the best we can do is begin treatments and take a 'wait and see' attitude."

You and your spouse are invited by the doctor to react.

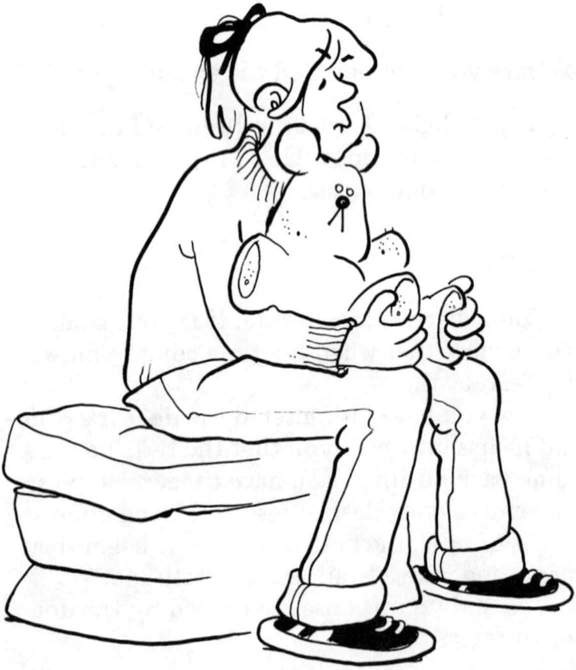

6. The Art of Living 'in the Midst of' the World

E

is for Environment

The experience of being in trouble can teach us much about ourselves and about the adolescents God has entrusted to our care. Let's see what we can learn by just carefully looking at the possible meanings of the simple phrase, "You are in trouble."

There is an important difference between being *in the midst of* trouble and being *in* trouble. In the first case, imagine yourself caught in a serious hotel fire: You are in a trouble-filled situation. In the second case, imagine yourself driving down the street, having just enthusiastically welcomed in the New Year, and seeing a flashing red light in your rear-view mirror. We have all experienced the differing emotions when we are faced with these two types of trouble.

In the case of the fire, you may see small children or elderly persons in danger and, at the risk of your own life, help them to safety. You may find yourself jumping three or four stories to an outstretched canvas held by your rescuers. You may dash back into the fire to save someone screaming for help. You may momentarily panic, but soon your whole system tells you to *do something* and you do. You are aware that you are *in the midst of* trouble. You know that some action is needed to get out of the troublesome situation.

In the second type of trouble, you see yourself and the trouble as one. In this second instance it is much more difficult to rise above the situation. You *are* the trouble and are less able to see an immediate course of action. The way you react may be very different from the heroic you that mustered all your resources to overcome the flames of the raging fire.

Why is this so? Figuring out the reason can help you unlock that mysterious door that slams shut when your adolescents get into what is commonly called "a rotten mood."

Your adolescents spend a considerable amount of their young lives in rotten moods. Today it is easy for me to write about being in a bad mood—because I am in one. All I have to do is describe what is happening inside of me.

I am in a rotten mood—but I feel good. Why? My rotten mood and I are not *one*. For this reason I am able to do something usually reserved for "good mood" days, namely, write.

I am *in the midst of* my rotten mood and am aware that I can and must do something to get out. The first step is to realize that I am *not* trapped. I am *not* a helpless victim of the mood.

I do not know where the mood came from, any more than the person in the hotel fire knows the origin of the flames. Speculation on whether this mood is caused by the dreariness of the day or my mother's stubborn refusal to allow me to determine my own bedtime when I was five years old is presently irrelevant.

I can see clearly at this moment that my job is to *do something*. If I enjoyed painting, I'd paint. Cooking, I'd cook. But I enjoy writing. So, I am writing.

For a long time I sat and looked at the keys of my typewriter and they merely looked like alphabet soup. Nothing came. Every thought wanted to go back and dwell on the mood.

I said no. I said no to the debilitating mood the way the fire victim said no to standing inoperative in the midst of the flames. Today I am keenly aware that there is an *I* that *can* say no. So now I am writing.

As I write my mood is changing. *I* am remaining the same. My *mood* is changing.

Like clouds passing by, some moods are gray, some black, or bright, or silver-lined. But we must try to remember they are all moods *out there*. As we do not allow a rainy day to shatter us when we had outdoor plans, we must not allow a mood to control us.

My rotten mood is not controlling me today. Unlike the man staring helplessly into his rearview mirror, I am not *in* a mood. I am, rather, *aware* of a mood and have consciously chosen not to be *in* it.

Some days it takes me a long time to get to this awareness. On those days I am more my adolescent self. Then, until I get in touch with my adult self, I am trapped in a mood.

This sense of "being trapped" is exactly what happens to teenagers when they get "into a mood." Because they have gotten *into* it, they are stuck. This process of getting into the mood of the moment is much like reading and rereading old love letters searching for clues to the collapse of the relationship. Dwelling on the letters, like dwelling on the mood, only makes it worse. Such concentration intensifies the mood.

You, as parents, can really help your adolescents out of their moods. Your first step is to help them see that they *can* get out. They are not in bondage to a passing tyrannical mood.

You, of course, cannot pull them out of their mood. You want to help because of the obvious pain they are in. Unfortunately you cannot help them shake their mood by external coercion such as, "Come on, snap out of it. You've been dragging around here all day."

Nor does the magic of kind understanding usually help: "I understand how you feel; it isn't all that bad."

The teenager in a mood knows it is his or her own mood and that you cannot possible understand. The moody person alone has the key to unlock his or her particular trapdoor. All you can do is encourage your adolescents to remember that they can help themselves.

Pushing Toward the Center

In order for your adolescents to help themselves out of a mood they must become *centered*.

Only a centered person can overcome a mood rather than be overcome by it.

A centered person acts from his or her center. This type of authentic activity demands that a person know his or her true self.

Once we *know* our self, we must then learn to *accept* the self we now know. The temptation, like the temptation that confronted Adam and Eve, is to reject our true self in favor of an "idea"—the way we ought to be, the way we think we are. We still want to be like gods—flawless. Once we do accept our true self, with its nobility and its negative aspects, we must learn to love that true self.

Becoming centered, therefore, is not easy. For most of us it is the full-time work of our life on this planet.

The person who is not centered, who never discovers his or her uniqueness, ends up like Charles Schultz's classic character Charlie Brown. Because Charlie lacks conviction, inner principles, he is labeled "wishy-washy." Charlie does not know what he stands for on any issue.

Until your adolescents know, accept and love their true selves, they are wishy-washy too. Because they do not know what they stand for, they easily fall for everything. You can help them to their feet by consistently calling your adolescents' uniqueness forth. Help them measure their "ideas," what they *think*, against what they *know* inside.

Each of us arrives at our center at differing speeds. Some people seem to die while still "on edge." Others seem to *know* from a very early age. Paul Harvey recently reported that an 85-year-old blind man, living alone, killed himself. He left a scribbled note stating, "I can see no other way."

Had this poor man reached into his center a different path might have opened before his inner eyes. If this man had a "parent" in the form of a friend to call him forth from his despairing mood, he might still be alive and filled with joy.

To find this joy in living, all the philosophers and sages advise one thing: Know thyself. In this knowledge of self, we learn how to live, how to become our very best self.

Since we all want to be our very best self, we are constantly searching for that inner truth. This search has led some to mountaintops, some to monasteries. Some have traveled the path of psychic phenomena. Many try to meet their self through the help of psychiatry. And, of course, this searching has taken many down the temporarily appealing roads of drugs, disco delirium and drink. Whatever the path an adolescent chooses, he or she wants, from the very core, to become an authentic self.

Until your adolescents do become themselves, they are victims of this world as they are of their moods. They become confused and think they are living *in* the world and are not aware that they are merely *in the midst of* it. Until your adolescent is able to make the important distinction between being *in* the world and *in the midst of* the world, he or she experiences serious psychological growing pains.

As parents you can help your sons and daughters remember that they are not "wishy-washy." They need not be pushed around by circumstances. They can act *on* their environment.

Unfortunately your adolescents' real selves are forgotten during much of their pain-filled young lives. They are so distracted by their thoughts or the passing parade of sensual delights, they hardly have time to be *with* their true self.

Being *with* our self demands silence and solitude. Silence does not mean turning off the radio, but quieting the mind. Solitude does not mean physical isolation, but an awareness of our very isolated unique self even in the midst of Grand Central Station.

The glitter that the present generation has grown up with militates against self-knowledge and keeps them *outside* themselves. Your work as parent is to keep them going *within*—deeper and deeper each day. This pushing them toward their center, their truth, demands that you be pulling from in front. They cannot follow your example if you are not in the lead. So really, to parent properly, you must be working primarily on becoming centered yourself.

Living in the Truth

To work on yourself demands the same discipline that you impose on your adolescents when they are "not themselves." The discipline is, simply, the truth. You must always check out what you *think* against what you *know*. If you follow your deepest knowledge, you will always and in every situation be able to lead your children effectively.

So when you *think* the reason you are tired is because of a hard day at the office but *know* that your tiredness comes from another source, discipline is needed. A dose of the truth is needed. You know your exhaustion comes from mentally fighting all day with your spouse because of a remark passed at breakfast.

Do not take the "thoughtful" way out. It does not work. You will continue the battle in your sleep. Walk in the truth and talk with your spouse about your perception. The air will clear in less than 30 seconds. You might then have the energy to go dancing—or at least have a good night's sleep.

To shirk our responsibility to live in the truth is adolescent. Being adolescent means subjecting ourselves to what is happening *out there.* We are victims of moods, thoughts, others' words.

An adult is not a victim, nor is he or she concerned with winning victories. An adult wants to know the truth. By living in the truth, an adult brings healing to situations torn by the clashing of individualistic perceptions of reality.

When we do live in the truth—that is, become adult—we gain some control over two very negative aspects of our adolescent personalities: adolescent competition and the dubious art of "put-down."

Competition is a good thing, if it is *good* competition. Most competition, however, is not good—it is adolescent. Adolescent competition demands the existence of underdogs or losers. In football and basketball, adolescent competition may be harmless because the games come to an end. Adolescent competition in the game of life, however, is dangerous and destructive.

Overcoming Adolescent Competition

Adolescent competition is played by people who do not know that they are okay. They do not know, love and accept their unique selves. The only rule the adolescent competitor follows is this: Anything goes in order to remain on top—to remain number one. Because adolescent competitors do not know they are okay, they think winning makes others think they are great.

The day people *know* in their hearts they are okay, adolescent competition ceases. They know that they are okay and so is everyone else. With this knowledge, the competitor is ready for real, adult competition—the adult competition that God intended the day he decided to create us as multi-talented human beings.

Competition comes from two Latin words: *cum*, with, and *peto*, I beg. Literally then, we are beggars with each other. None of us has anything. All we have, we have received from a generous benefactor. The best things in life we have all won by working together, not in opposition. Real competition has brought us the classic plays in sports, not the singular efforts of the classic "hotdogger." The triple play demands that several persons "do their thing" very well, *together*.

The same holds for music. The best music results when the orchestra, soloist and conductor each use a unique gift well, together.

Great athletes and great musicians all know that teamwork is just another way of saying they are "begging together." The voice, the strong throwing arm are all gifts from God.

Once the conductor *knows* that he is the conductor, his adolescent competition ceases. He does not want to be the soloist. He has no fear that the soloist will want or be able to replace him. The conductor will feel no jealousy. He will rejoice in the talent of the rest.

Unlike great musicians and athletes, your adolescents do not know they are special. They do not know they have unique gifts shared by no other human being. And since they want desperately to be someone, someone they think they ought to be, they do not know the someone they are.

For this reason adolescents live emulating heroes, usually those canonized by an adolescent society. So your sons or daughters spend much time wanting to be *like* someone else—a someone they think is better than they because that someone is richer, or prettier, or famous. Sadly, by attempting to be someone they can never be, your teenagers establish some very *self*-defeating goals.

An adult has personal goals that spring from his or her *within*. Therefore the goals are realizable. An adult, therefore, has only one hero: his or her authentic self.

Because adults know that only they can do

the unique thing they were sent to this planet to do, an adult rejoices in the unique "thing-doing" of others. Only adolescents are threatened when another does his or her "own thing."

The ill effects of adolescent competition are many. When such competition is the energizing force in society, we see the multiplication of shelves filled with useless products in competition with each other. We see the humiliating—and frightening—need for nuclear weaponry to protect *us* from *them*. We see the growth of conformity.

Real competition, adult competition, eliminates conformity. Conformity is an act of cowardice.

Overcoming the 'Put-Down'

The second personality factor that disappears when we get to know our true selves is the "put-down." Once people know they are irreplaceable, they no longer need to keep others down.

Put-downs can be funny. Put-downs are frequently the meat of a comic routine. One prima donna speaks to another: "Who did your make-up, darling? Emmett Kelly?"

Put-downs can be cruel. The cruel put-downs are the ones that cut us to the core of our personal life, our family life.

The put-downs that we hear from friends and family are not so blatant as the comic one above; nor are they funny. Here is an example: "Heard you won first place in the tennis tournament at the club. *I was surprised.*" Gotcha!

When we discover our true self, we will experience control over our environment. We will not be pushed around by external events. We will not need to rearrange reality to make us look good in the eyes of our fellow "competitors." Our unique "I" will live *in the midst of* the world. In the turmoil of life, we will have someone inside remaining constant. Being in touch with our inner truth, *centered*, we will act uniquely in each of life's situations. We will have stopped trying to be someone else.

As parents, you are faced with an awesome responsibility. You must become your truest self so you can guide your adolescent. Let me remind you, you do have the ability. Some days will be easy—when you are adult. Others will be difficult—when you are adolescent yourself. On adult days you can parent. On adolescent days you will be tempted to compete or put down. Remember you are not perfect. But you, best of all, know how to raise your particular children. This is why God gave them to *you*.

Goethe, a German poet, wrote: "The moment you trust yourself, you will know how to live." Trust yourself, your *self*, and you and your family will have life, life in abundance.

Heart-to-Heart Discussion Starters

1) When you find yourself in a rotten mood, what ways do you use to pull yourself out of it?

2) Have you ever felt forced to compete in an adolescent way?

3) Why do we fear *adult* competition? What do we feel we will lose if we compete adultly? Why do we gain more from adult competition than from adolescent competition?

4) Can you think of times you have put others down? Why do you do this?

5) What are the pressures in society to conform?

An Experiment

Have someone in the group read the directions while the rest follow them. The purpose of this experiment is to experience the "I" that lives in the midst of the world and cannot be pushed around by your environment.

1) Directions:
   a) Close your eyes.
   b) Point to your left eye.
   c) Point to your nose.
   d) Point to your right or left elbow.
   e) Now point to your *self*.

2) Some reflections:
   a) Did you have difficulty pointing to your

self? Can your *self* be located in your head or heart?
b) Who is doing the pointing? And to push it further, when thinking, who is doing the thinking?
c) Share your reactions to the experiment.

7. The Art of Separating Wants From Needs

N
is for Needs

What we need and what we *think* we need are often two different things. We frequently consider them to be the same. Overweight persons, for example, are walking proof that people can think they need more than they do.

We get a clue as to how this confusion affects our daily lives by listening closely to our speech. Frequently we hear a person state, "When I wake up in the morning, I need a brisk cup of coffee before I can move." Yet in an emergency that same person can leap from bed and break the world's record for the 100-yard dash.

I used to comment that I needed a full five minutes to adjust in the morning before standing up. This was usually said to contrast myself with those energetic persons who bound from their beds at the crack of dawn. I was forced to eat my words the day the great earthquake hit Los Angeles in the early 1970's. During that 60-second tremor I made it from my second-floor room to the kitchen before the shaking stopped.

It took an earthquake to convince me that I misused the word *need*. I *want* to sit on the edge of my bed for five minutes and pamper myself into an upright position. But for a grown man to make such an admission to the world at large, even to myself, seemed too overwhelming. It was easier to say, "I need."

Who could begrudge me my *needed* time? It is as if I said I needed insulin. Who would keep me from my daily dose? But the day you find out that I do not really need insulin, but use it as an excuse to get out of work, you can and will become angry.

To avoid such anger directed at my morning sloth, I'd rather camouflage my want under the guise of a need. This is a way of avoiding responsibility for human weaknesses. It is a way of looking perfect in the eyes of others.

It takes a psychological adult to identify wants. One must also be adult to know what he or she actually needs. Because your son or daughter is caught in that in-between time, they seldom know what they need and rarely can say what they want. By looking at your own insides, you will see that frequently you are caught in the same adolescent dilemma.

Our actual needs are relatively few. People who are taken from their comfortable homes and forced to survive under disaster conditions learn that. Our wants, however, are many. Most of the time when we say *need*, we are doubletalking. We are really expressing a want.

What do small children want? They want everything that attracts their attention. They want "all that glitters." What do they need? Their parents *know*, and a good parent will not give into all of their children's wants.

When does a five-year-old *want* an ice cream cone? Whenever possible. When does she *need* it? Possibly never. When does she get one? When her parent decides. This decision takes into consideration the child's dental report and weight, as well as the family petty cash. Sometimes all of these elements are overlooked by a parent because of a deeper need. The child may *need* a treat.

As children move into adolescence, their wants do not die. In adolescence, however, people can start taking responsibility for *when* they really need what they want.

The signal to examine a want comes from one's inner *Parent.* Frequently an adolescent relinquishes this responsibility to flesh-and-blood parents.

When teenagers announce they do not want to go to school, they know before anything is said that they are acting like a child. When something is said they act indignant: "Don't you think I know that already? I know I cannot skip school." You may be tempted to say, "But you just said. . ." Deliver yourself from that temptation. Just know that they do know.

Your adolescents understand that they cannot always have what they want. They know what is good and not good for them to have at the same moment you do. The difference is they don't have the strength to discipline themselves. So they make *you* discipline them. How? By saying something that will infuriate you even though they are not sure why you are so angry.

Let's look at an example of how this interaction works. Your son rises each school morning at 5 a.m. to go swimming in order to improve his position on the school swim team. On Saturday morning you try to arouse him from his slumber to begin cleaning the garage. You call. You call again. You enter the room and shake the bed. You call. Shake. You yell. He responds, "I can't get up. I *need* more sleep."

He obviously has the discipline for something he wants. Where is the discipline for something you want?

The day your adolescent—or your own adolescent self—begins to say what is wanted, uncamouflaged, a first step to maturity is taken. But that means you and your adolescent must be able to separate real needs from wants.

The Biggest Need: Approval

What do adolescents actually need? Sometimes they need some of their childish wants fulfilled. Self-discipline or external discipline will determine when. But what does an adolescent need to gain the strength to move into adulthood? The answer is approval.

Since your adolescents do not feel okay about themselves, they need your approval, your praise, your affirmation. This real need will last until they are able to approve themselves from within.

Because of this need for external approval, an important part of a teenager's high school curriculum is what the rest of us consider "extra." Sports, drama, clubs—all extracurriculars play an essential part in the overall picture of academic life. Learning math may help young people in the world of work, but learning that they are okay will help them live.

With adolescents, flattery will get them *somewhere*. The somewhere is the place we call "adult." You cannot praise a teenager enough. This is not pride on their part, but a need that comes from a lack of self-love.

You can rejoice that you are the one able to give these necessary emotional vitamins most effectively. Just as you have witnessed physical growth from the food you have fed your children, you will see emotional growth if you make sure they do not develop "compliment-deficiency." The more complimentary you can be the better.

Adults who are fully mature also have needs. But a mature adult's needs are simple. A mature adult, because he or she does have a good self-concept, does not need external approval. A mature adult likewise does not have to camouflage wants as needs as children do. A psychologically mature adult can simply say, "I want to smoke," rather than, "I need a cigarette."

We must remember that when we are speaking of an adult who is fully integrated, we are speaking of a rare individual.

Much of the time we so-called adults are psychologically adolescent. During these times we, like teenagers, need praise. We need compliments. We need others to approve our existence on this earth. On our adult days we do not *need* compliments but merely *enjoy* them.

Our adolescent behavior embarrasses us so we deny that we still have this need for the approval of others. Denial is dangerous, however, because, like an actual teenager, we must see our pseudo-needs for what they are—our wants.

For example, a person might be deeply hurt if his or her name is mistakenly left off the "volunteer" plaque placed in the hospital corridor. Why be hurt if the volunteering was really voluntary? Most behavior is not so simple. We do much of whatever we do for recognition.

An adult must say, "I want": "I want the approval of my community. I am helping at the hospital so others will notice, as well as because I want to help others." The day we recognize this fact, embarrassing as it is, we begin the process of approving ourselves. We see how silly it is to need the approval of others and, somehow, that very recognition helps us grow.

When your adolescent boy says that he needs to get a varsity letter, he does. When your daughter says she needs to be a member of the queen's court, she does. At this stage of life, they do need what brings them the approval of others.

A child of two or 102 does not know that what he or she *wants* will not bring happiness. Adolescents of 17 or 77 do not know that external approval does not make them okay. Only an adult knows what makes him or her happy; only an adult knows what it means to be approved "as is."

An adult knows that happiness comes from wanting what God wants in any given situation. What the adult might *want* is not necessarily what he or she *needs* to grow. So an adult learns to *listen.* An adult knows that a loving God will send what is needed for growth. One day it will be a pat on the back, another a kick in the backside.

As parents you need to remember that if you, weak as you are, know how to give the good things to fill your children's needs, what of God? You know how to say no when needed to your son or daughter who will "die" if not allowed to stay out all night. You know how to give them things they do need even when they are unaware.

Because of this knowledge it is possible for you as parents to understand why Jesus taught his disciples to pray in this way: "Give us this day our daily bread." Give us, that is, what we need, not what we think, like children, we need. Not what we need like adolescents because we still don't believe God loves us as we are.

Heart-to-Heart Discussion Starters

1) Some religions and many individuals hold that sickness is mentally induced, that illness is an excuse to avoid some responsibility. Do you believe this? If this were true, explain how many of your adolescent's "sicknesses" could be traced to "avoidance of responsibility." Cite examples.

2) Beatlemania began with four young men from Liverpool, England, who obviously had very good self-concepts. Explain this statement.

3) Is it easy for you to compliment your adolescents? Do they take well to praise?

4) How do you react to compliments? Are you embarrassed? What does your reaction tell you about yourself?

5) Are you able to give yourself permission to enjoy "the things of a child" even though you no longer *need* them? Do you feel it is good to give in to childish desires now and then?

6) Do you feel it is too idealistic to trust that God will send you your daily needs?

7) What is wrong with the concept: "God helps those who help themselves?" Anything? Everything? Explain.

8) What implications do you see for the handicapped, the weak, uneducated and aged in

the philosophy that God will only help those capable of lending God a helping hand? Do you see any examples of this philosophy in our present day?

Role Play

Unexpected guests arrive on New Year's Day. Your husband and two teenage sons are very involved in watching football. You request the TV be turned off since it is in the living room. Your sons storm out and go to a neighbor's to watch the game. Your husband remains and pouts. Your husband's reactions are obvious to both you and your guests. React.

1) What TA transactions were occurring?

2) How could your husband have acted differently?

3) How could you have acted differently in the situation?

4) What measures can you take to decrease the possibility of such an incident in the future?

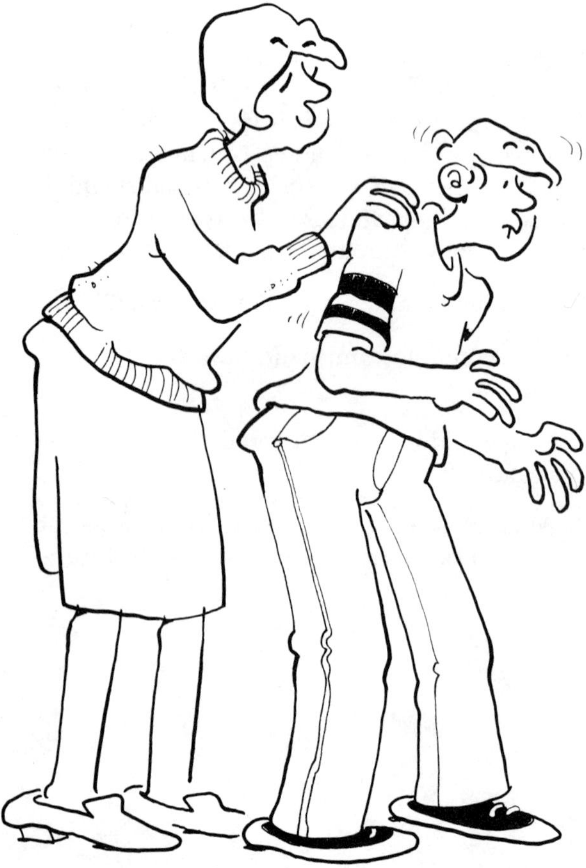

8. The Art of Being God's Instrument

T
is for Touch

When Jesus met someone who was ill or dead, he touched them. By his touch miraculous things happened. The lame walked. The deaf heard. The dead rose to life.

To think that Jesus' physical hand caused the miracle is to think that a paint brush in the hands of Michelangelo caused the painting. The paint brush is an instrument; Jesus' hand is an instrument. The picture, the healing are the results of instruments used by a spirit in touch with the divine.

Your arms are instruments. They can be used

to squeeze to death or hug to life. They can be used to keep people at a distance or to draw someone close to you. The way you use your arms in the rearing of your adolescent children will depend on how in touch you are with the divine.

Your parental heart might best be described as a roaring furnace. But your children are cold. They feel isolated, afraid. The world, even with its appearance of warmth, always leaves them cold. This is why they have you: a father who can continuously give new life, a mother who can keep that life secure. But the fire of your love cannot be seen unless you demonstrate it. For this reason you have been given a pair of arms.

This divine power that you have—to heal, to quicken, to give life—is all too often short-circuited. Your love comes back upon itself not because you do not want to give it to your sons and daughters, but because you do not know how. Or because you will not risk rejection.

Rejection is a common fear among parents, because parents are human beings and this is *the* common fear of humankind. Who among us has a strong enough self-appreciation not to fear being rejected? Very few, and those very few are the totally integrated among us, the adults.

Even when you are adult you have your non-adult moments. During your non-adult periods you are deeply hurt if someone turns you off, puts you down, makes a crack or a cutting remark, or laughs. During these times you are vulnerable. During these vulnerable periods you are identical to your adolescent who lives in this sensitive emotional zone 24 hours a day. At these sensitive times your love is locked under a thick layer of fear.

Fortunately these periods do not last forever. You do have days and weeks when you know you are okay. During these times you have the strength to unleash the God-given power of your heart. If your teenage boy laughs when you go to hug him, you can smile knowingly. It is his problem. He does not feel okay and therefore feels silly when hugged. Your persistence will one day make him feel better about himself and the silly feeling will subside.

The days you cannot hug, because you fear that laugh, will help you further understand your adolescent sons and daughters. Your feeling is a good reminder of their emotional state. They are embarrassed because they do not feel worthy of your affection.

Only on a terribly off-day, when you feel equally unworthy, do you think this means they do not love you. Look at the glint in their eyes, not the push in their arms. Their eyes tell you they love the attention but just now are unable to accept it.

Sensitive to your teenager's inability to accept such overt attention, you might try the "backdoor" approach. This approach allows the recipient of your affection to think that no one notices. I vividly remember the day a mother of one of my junior boys came running across the school yard screaming excitedly, "It worked!"

I had mentioned the back-door approach at a parents' night. I told the parents it would work, but honestly I only *thought* so. Her experiment with the back-door approach validated my hypothesis, so now I *know*. Here is her story:

"I started a week ago," she told me. "You said it would be slow going so I figured it would take much longer than one small week. Anyway, here is what happened. I walked up to Jeff last Monday and, as usual when he saw my arms coming, he winced. I was in a good space, Father, and excited about trying the new approach. I put my hand ever so lightly on his shoulder, the one nearest me. I gave his shoulder a pat and walked away. I could not see, but felt, his wide-eyed expression, his 'where-is-my-mother-the-tackle' look.

"Tuesday I did the same; the same result. Wednesday I gave him a prolonged 'shoulder message.' Thursday, a pat on the back. By Friday I was around the bend, with my arm around his shoulders, and Saturday and Sunday my race with fear was over. Now when I give Jeff a hug, he acts like it is normal, not strange."

Your adolescents want to be hugged. They need it. Hugging is a very concrete sign of approval. Don't let fear keep you apart.

Knowing how and when to keep in physical touch will demand that you keep in touch on a more profound level. You, as parent, must keep in touch with the present moment.

Paying Attention to the Here-and-Now

"Present moment" is another way of saying *reality*. All else—the past, the future, whether we are talking about time or our thinking—does not exist.

The Second World War is over. A person who dwells on it constantly as if it were still happening is mentally ill. The future, the possible Third World War, is not real either. A person who spends his or her days worrying about that event is also mentally ill. The mentally healthy person, the most *human* human being is the one who lives in the *here-and-now*. The parent who is disciplined to live in the here-and-now makes the best parent.

The reason is simple: Such a parent can be present to the actual needs of a child. A small child may need just one more kiss before retiring. The parent who remembers the child's grouchy behavior at Grandma's or is aware of a big day tomorrow may miss that here-and-now.

The parent of an adolescent parents better by keeping in touch with the present moment, too. The unique individual that stands before you at any given moment cannot be seen from memory. He or she cannot be viewed from the perspective of the future either.

The adolescent who is asking for the car keys today is not the one who asked yesterday or will ask tomorrow. You must be alert, attentive. Yesterday this was a two-year-old asking for the keys. You, alert to that here-and-now, said no, and rightly so. Today you face a responsible young adult; saying no may be a harmful answer. Tomorrow will have to wait until tomorrow.

For you to pay attention is another way—an effective way—to put your arms around your adolescent. The love they feel when you hold them is repeated when you hold their words as sacred. The very fact that you pay attention tells them in a very special way that you feel they are okay. Someday you will see them pay attention to themselves. On that day they will say less, know more, and return your love a hundredfold.

Your parental heart, then, is a pulsating furnace of love. Your sons and daughters need to *know* love, not merely think they are lovable. With physical embraces and with attentive listening you will be able to keep in touch and convey this love God gave you to give to them.

For you to give to your adolescents what you already have, you must become an instrument of God. You must be in touch with the divine. If you do become this divine instrument, you will bring his healing to your children. No area of an adolescent's life need remain an open wound when tended by such a glorious physician.

Tuning In to God

To be this healer, this divine instrument, you must be your best adult self as much of the time as possible. To be your best self, you must let go of who you think you are, what you think you want, what you think is best for your children, yourself and the world as a whole. You must tune in to a divine signal.

Quieting your thinking mind and entering into the silence where your heart leads the way may help. The methods of meditation vary and you can find your own. But meditation is not a luxury for a parent. Whether you spend 15 minutes morning and night in a chapel or on your knees, or find yourself thinking things over as you stir a cup of coffee, you *must* meditate. Meditation merely means you stop thinking so you can see what is really happening and be present to it.

We can learn a great deal about the true meaning of love—and that includes that unique thing called parental love—from Saint Francis of Assisi. Francis never sired a son but his heart was a pure channel of divine love. By this love he gave spiritual birth to millions. Francis' famous prayer—which might well become your daily prayer—describes the perfect parent:

> Lord, make me an instrument of Your peace;
> Where there is hatred, let me sow love;
> where there is injury, pardon;
> where there is doubt, faith;
> where there is despair, hope;
> where there is darkness, light;
> and where there is sadness, joy.
>
> O Divine Master, grant that I may not so much seek to be consoled as to console;
> to be understood as to understand,

> to be loved as to love;
> for it is in giving that we receive,
> it is in pardoning that we are pardoned,
> and it is in dying that we are born
> > to eternal life.

You are not perfect. You are weak. You are all too human. Your weakness does not come from lack of strength, but lack of faith. Be compassionate with yourself. You want to love, but fail. You want to be understanding, but fail. You want to give, but take. When sadness pervades your spirit because of the weakness you see within yourself, think of the little Poor Man of Assisi.

Francis was a saint—when he died. Until then he was a struggling human being like you. Like me. He daily faced his own inadequacies, fears, failure. Take strength from him. Take strength as you parent your children. Take strength from the fact that Francis the human being did not say, "I *am* an instrument of your peace," but rather, "Lord, *make* me. . ."

Heart-to-Heart Discussion Starters

1) Describe your feelings when you have not been paid attention to. For example, how would you feel if, at a cocktail party, your host always looks over your shoulder for more interesting guests?

2) Who makes you feel most important in your daily life?

3) Do you feel comfortable in touching your teenagers?

4) Has touch been a part of your upbringing?

5) Do you have a method of staying present to the here-and-now? Share.

Role Play

Your teenager comes to you panicked about the upcoming S.A.T. tests that are so vital for college. Give some helpful advice.

Books to Help Parents on Their Way

The only bibliography that can satisfy your heart is the one you assemble. Different books speak to different people. Books that are rich food for one person leave another still hungering. If, however, one of the following selections does speak to you, cherish it.

These selections have helped me in my own struggle to grow up. I pass them on to you.

I. Fr. John Powell, a psychologist teaching at Loyola University in Chicago, has written a remarkable series of books incorporating both Transactional Analysis (TA) and spiritual principles. His books are easy reading. So if you feel the need to understand further the psychological dynamics of your own particular within, you might find his books helpful. The ones most helpful to me have been: **Why Am I Afraid to Tell You Who I Am?** (Argus), **Why Am I Afraid to Love?** (Argus), **The Secret of Staying in Love** (Argus).

II. If you need a book to guide you in meditation, try the excellent but simple book entitled: **Journey of Awakening: A Meditator's Guidebook,** by Ram Dass (Bantam Books).

This book is greatly influenced by the spiritual teachings of the East, but equally so by those of the West. There is tremendous food for a searching heart in this book.

III. For profound reflections on life, you may find very helpful a book which is ever new: **New Seeds of Contemplation,** by Thomas Merton (New Directions Books).

The now-famous Trappist monk, Thomas Merton, is one of our best guides in the traditions of Western Spirituality. If you know nothing of Thomas Merton, you might begin by reading his autobiography, **Seven Storey Mountain.**

IV. A book that speaks directly to a seeker's heart is **Poustinia,** by Catherine Doherty (Ave Maria Press). The word *poustinia* is Russian for "hermitage." If you have a thirst for God, a deep longing that seems unsatisfied, this book may well be for you.

V. If you need inspiration, you need to experience the life of St. Francis. Try the beautiful book: **Francis: The Journey and the Dream,** by Murray Bodo, O.F.M. (St. Anthony Messenger Press).

Father Bodo has stepped into the shoes of St. Francis. He feels Francis' struggle to become a spiritual adult. And since the struggle is the same for us, Father Bodo's words speak to us all.

VI. There are a host of books available on psychology, child-rearing and self-help. Only you can tell what is right for you. So spend an hour or so at your local bookstore looking through this tremendous storehouse of humanity's recorded search for understanding.

Here are but two I particularly like:

Your Child's Self-Esteem, by Dorothy Corkille Briggs (Doubleday). A very readable book with beautiful insights into how to help your growing child feel his or her self-worth. Chapter 17 is of special interest since it deals directly with the period of adolescence.

Peoplemaking, by Virginia Satir (Science and Behavior Books). This is a classic and is enormously helpful in understanding the way family members relate. Very important concepts are dealt with, such as nurturing communication. The book is easy to read and extremely practical in its approach.

VII. The most important book, of course, is the Scriptures. *The* adult man, equal to the Father, is Jesus of Nazareth. Jesus has given us much advice regarding the art of growing up. He has told us how we must die to our selfishness and shows us the way to rise to new life. If you have only a little time to read, spend that time wisely: Read what God has said to us in his Word-made-flesh.